Janeah Rose

REFLECTIONS OF A
PSYCHIC

TRUSTING YOUR INNER VOICE

Reflections of a Psychic: Trusting Your Inner Voice

by Janeah Rose

Copyright © 2012 Janeah Rose. All Rights Reserved. Printed in the United States of America. Excerpt as permitted under the United States Copyright Act of 1976, no part of this publication may be reproduced or distributed in any form, or by any means, or stored in a database retrieval system, without the prior written permission of the copyright holder, except by a reviewer, who may quote brief passages in review.

Neither the publisher nor the author is engaged in rendering advice or services to the individual reader. Neither the author nor the publisher shall be liable or responsible for any loss, injury, or damage allegedly arising from any information or suggestion in this book. The opinions expressed in this book represent the personal views of the author and not of the publisher, and are for informational purposes only.

This is a work of nonfiction. The events and experiences detailed herein are all true and have been faithfully rendered as the author has remembered them to the best of her ability. Some of the various stories of people in this book draw from a composite of stories. In some instances people's names have been changed in these stories to protect privacy and/or anonymity of the persons involved.

ISBN 978-0-9881171-0-5 - perfectbound

ISBN 978-0-9881171-1-2 - ePub

I have not written to discredit any beliefs, religions, credos or philosophies. It is about our own spiritual journey, what we may or may not believe, no matter what that may entail. Some of us believe we are supposed to stay happy with whatever cards we are dealt in life. While others believe that when there is a turn in the road, they must take it to discover what might be out there. I am a true believer that when you are fully engaged in the present moment, and become conscious of your emotions, you align your personality with your soul, and therefore are very open to change, adventure, happiness and good health, and are not afraid to move forward. The stories you are about to read are those people who were definitely at the turn in the road, were in tune with their emotions, and were ready to embrace whatever the universe was going to put in front of them...

Acknowledgements

Thanks to all my clients who have trusted and honored me. I thank you from the bottom of my heart for allowing me to be your guide and mentor. I feel deeply blessed to have had each and every one of you come through my life. You know who you are. You have been my source of inspiration and, if it weren't for you, and your stories there would be no book.. They are confirmation of your true essences, and my gift of Intuition

Thanks to my partner Keith who has been so encouraging, supportive and understanding. While I've been pounding away on the keyboard at all hours of the night, you have been trying to get some sleep. I promise one day the kitchen table will be cleared of all the paraphernalia and trappings that have commandeered living space. The reign of my journals, diaries, letters, and notes written to myself in the early morning hours—will soon be taking a sabbatical and you will once again be able to see your place mat. I know it's buried under there somewhere!

Thanks to my brother Nat who continues to motivate me with all of his unbelievable enthusiasm! All of your research on agents, publishers, editors, marketing agents, magazines and advertizing, has all been tucked away and filed under 'Nat's Book Info'. You continue to amaze me, but most of all, you inspire me.

Thanks to my sisters Julie and Rose/ Susie for believing in me! As sisters your encouraging words mean the world to me. As a psychic reader, your trust in me makes me feel proud. As a writer, your encouragement makes it all worth while.

Thanks to my mom who has the sharp memory to recall all the fascinating little details of my growing-up years as a small child. You are so much a part of all my childhood memories, and I feel blessed to still have you in my life sharing them together over tea.

Thank-you to my editor Dennis Mullen at *Havana Writers' Retreat* for the many long hours of editing along with your continued support and enthusiasm for this book.

Thanks as well to all the readers of my first book, *Finding Happiness without Children*. I so much appreciated all of your emails, testimonials, letters and phone calls. They have all motivated me even further to continue writing.

Table of Contents

Prelude: How to Get The Most Out Of This Book xi
Foreword. xiii
Chapter 1: My First Clear Vision 1
Chapter 2: Accepting Criticism 10
Chapter 3: Ouija Boards. 19
Chapter 4: Finding My True Purpose 27
Chapter 5: Psychic Expectations 37
Chapter 6: The Ultimate Lesson 39
Chapter 7: Proving Myself To Sceptics 43
Chapter 8: Trusting My Inner Voice. 52
Chapter 9: Quality Time With Father. 68
Chapter 10: Once In A Lifetime 73
Chapter 11: Angel Intervention 92
Chapter 12: Miracles Really Do Happen 104
Chapter 13: My Biggest Sceptic 126
Chapter 14: Never Say Never 138
Chapter 15: Love-Struck in the Desert 150
Chapter 16: The Greatest Gift Of All 163
Chapter 17: When the Path Is Clear. 176
Chapter 18: Have A Little Faith 187
Chapter 19: The Winners 195
Chapter 20: North To Alaska 205
Chapter 21: Worst Case Scenario 215
Chapter 22: The Wedding That Wasn't to Be 226
Chapter 23: The Search For A Daughter 237
Chapter 24: The Murder 252

Prelude

How to Get The Most Out Of This Book

My intention in writing this book is to open people's minds to the eternity of life, so everyone can enrich, explore and enlighten their own life by the magic and miraculous energy that surrounds all of us, in our own everyday life. No matter who, or what your religion or credo is, we are all made up of energy.

These stories are based on my own true personal and professional experiences over the last thirty-five years. They are about ordinary people, who lead ordinary lives, some of which were non believers in the psychic phenomenon, but were curious as to what might be in store for them. Many were at a cross road, while others were content but needed confirmation. Some needed guidance and assurance that they were making the right choices. These stories have been taken from my collection of journals and diaries, and were documented as some of the most profound, unbelievable, heart-warming, miraculous, and magical stories that have patiently been waiting until the time was right for publishing.

I believe that now is the right time, as more and more people these days are searching for answers, wanting to know if they are on the right path.

"Will I ever find my true purpose? And, "How will I know *when* I have found it? These are some of the very questions that I am asked on a daily basis. People—who previously never believed in paranormal phenomena—are now searching out any form of gifted liaison through psychic readers, hypnotists, regression therapists, self-help books, and the list goes on.

We all need to have confirmation, validation, clarity, and happiness surrounding our decisions. And if going to find the answers with a well known gifted psychic can help make you feel better about yourself, your choices, or your future, then this is a great way to have confirmation as well as fun, adventure and very often life changing experiences.

One of my aspirations in writing this book is that it will influence non-believers and shatter some, if not all, of the myths that may have influenced their way of thinking towards psychics. Hopefully these stories will cause them to look at life—maybe even their own life—differently, so that they too can reach all of their goals by simply believing in themselves, listening to their own inner voice and growing spiritually. It's important to realize that psychics are just people with extraordinary gifts, and when we see or feel things, It is up to us to deliver the message in the best way we know how, even if it doesn't make sense to us at the time. I'm sure these stories will resonate in your heart as they did mine, and you will find yourself believing not only in intuition, but also in miracles, angels, the universe, destiny, fate and last but not least, our Creator.

Foreword

Growing up in a large Roman Catholic Italian middle-class family wasn't always easy, and like many big families in the '50s and '60s there were just as many happy times as there were bad. And, being as we didn't know any different, it made it a whole lot easier. Mind you, we learned at a very young age how to make due with very little. It wasn't until we were in our teens that we began to realize that we really were a lot poorer than we had thought. We began to notice that most of our friends had an allowance, their very own hairdresser, fancy clothes for every season, and shoes for every occasion—while mother was sewing patchwork blankets from old coats to keep us warm at night.

My mother, who was in her thirties when I was in my teens, and whom I thought was ancient—until I reached 25—was a stay at home mom, who was forever teaching us right from wrong, how to be honest, kind, giving and, most of all, how to respect our elders. She was born in the early '20s in Vancouver Canada, was from full blooded Italian parents, and was raised by her widowed mother of 13 children.   She married my father, who was 12 years her senior, at the age of 20. Dad was born in Italy and moved to Canada when he was just 3 years old. His background was very Catholic, and he was raised very strict in a family of only two children, where hard work was always the key to happiness. Dad worked as an industrial arts teacher and his passions were fishing, carpentry, and a fitness regimen consisting of running and exercise. He was an athletic enthusiast most of his life. His gold, silver and bronze medals for races he ran and won in the city of Vancouver in the '30s are a testament to that passion.

Both mom and dad were very intuitive, but were never encouraged to excel on it in any way shape or form. Being intuitive or psychic in those days, over 100 years ago now, was not a word they were familiar with, or wanted to learn about.... That is of coarse until many years later, when they happened to have a daughter, who was always experiencing unexplainable, uncanny, coincidences as they called it...

Our home was a comfortable three-story Victorian style design. We took it for granted how big and spacious it was, and looking back at pictures now, it reminds me of a house you would see in the movies of the Humphrey Bogart or Clark Gable. It boasted three huge bedrooms atop a winding staircase, where all seven siblings had ample room. My brothers shared a big bedroom directly beside us girls. We spent many a night playing *Monopoly* or *Pick-Up-Sticks*, while listening to country music by Hank Williams and Jim Reeves. Frank was my oldest brother who was the apple of my Dad's eye. Everywhere my Dad went Frank was sure to follow. Dad finally had someone to make a fishing-rod for, and someone to take fishing with him when mom was too busy with the younger children. Larry was second oldest and was the clown in the family—he had the uncanny ability to always make everyone laugh, even if they were in a bad mood. His magic tricks sometimes got me into hot

Foreword

water, as I believed everything he would try tricking me with. Like the time I was about six years old when he told me that I would get my wish and be able to grow a money tree if I planted a shinny penny in the ground. I remember every day faithfully taking a glass of water to the patch of ground where I planted the penny, watering it, and watching over it like a hawk, trying to find some sign of growth, and after several months of nothing except more weeds, and everyone wondering why I was watering the dirt, my brother confessed, "I was just joking"

Christmases seemed to encompass the most memorable times of my childhood. I was always thankful for all the little things; our mother spending endless hours knitting and crocheting scarves and mitts for us which kept us warm while playing in the snow on cold winter days, the delight of the Christmas tree resplendently decorated Christmas morning.

One of my fondest memories of a Christmas was when I was 7 years old. My two oldest brothers woke me up shortly after I fell asleep. The idea was to sneak out of bed and down the hall to the top of the stairs so we could wait for Santa to come down the chimney and watch him while he dispatched gifts under the Christmas tree, and to look into the dark sky, and watch for Santa and his Reindeer with the big sleigh full of presents. I really was the biggest believer in Santa Claus. I remember jumping out of bed like a bullet when it was still dark out, and running down the twenty-three stairs so fast that I tripped at the bottom, and went flying into the living room right in front of the most beautiful Christmas tree I'd ever seen in my life. I was so excited to see that Santa did find our house that I ran back up the stairs as fast as I came down yelling, "Wake up, wake up! You should see what Santa Claus brought for us—a whole bunch of presents for everybody!"

As I dragged mom and dad out of bed I remember them looking as surprised as I. They followed all of us sleepy eyed kids down the stairs, and sat with us while we all opened our gifts. It was 3AM! Colourfully wrapped presents scattered about glimmered in the soft aura of the Scotch pine's glowing lights. A shiny toy train-set sat gleaming on tracks at the base of the tree. An illuminated locomotive made its course around the tree all the while making the sounds of a real train. It was so fascinating for me. My brothers loved it. I remember wondering how Santa could have possibly carried such a big train-set upon his sled.

One of my favorite Christmas gifts' was when I was about seven years old. It was just a little book, in hard cover, called *Little Women*. For some strange and inexplicable reason, when I first opened this book I felt as though it had been mine before. I immediately became attached to it and seemed to carry it around with me everywhere I went. It felt as though I had read it before because I seemed to know what each page was going to say. At this particular time I was reading any book I could get my hands on just because it felt good reading a story on my own, without help from either my brothers or my mom and dad. I will admit though, that sometimes what I was reading didn't make a whole lot of sense, but this book made me feel as though I was the girl in the story. However, what turned out to be more interesting than the book was the bookmark that I found tucked in between the pages a few days later. It wasn't like most bookmarks you see today—it was turquoise-blue and pink, and the size of an ordinary playing card. It had lost most of its sheen and all four corners were bent. Overall, it was weathered looking. It had a picture of the Blessed Virgin Mary on the front but it wasn't until I was almost finished reading the book when I noticed something was written on the back. It was there I

Foreword

discovered the faded words "Listen and You Will Hear." It was handwritten in a fancy calligraphic script. The peculiar thing was that no one seemed to know who wrote it or, where the bookmark came from. The obvious first question—was it in the book right from the store or had someone put it in the book before mom wrapped it? Being inquisitive as always, I had to know what these words meant, so I asked my dad one night as he was replacing a light bulb in my bedroom.

Right out of the blue I asked, "Dad, what exactly does 'Listen and You Will Hear' mean?"

"Why do you ask?" he inquired, as he was coming down the ladder.

"Well, I'll show you the bookmark that was in the book I got for Christmas," I said, as I reached for it upon my night table. He took it from me as though it was some kind of lost treasure.

He first looked at the beautiful picture of the Blessed Virgin Mary, and said, "Do you know that I named you after the Blessed Virgin Mary?"

Looking at him with admiration as I always did, I answered, "No I didn't know that Dad."

He then turned it over and read it out loud. "Listen and You Will Hear. Hmmm." Thinking about it for a moment and then scratching his head he told me, "Well...I believe it is when you ask a question to God—and you listen closely and quietly—you will hear a voice."

"You will?" I asked, in disbelief. "Hear whose voice dad?"

His reply was one I have never forgotten. "You will hear a voice."

"*I* will hear a voice? I asked, wanting to know more.

He answered just before turning my bedroom light off, "Yes, and if you listen carefully, you will be able to decide for yourself whose voice it is."

"What do you mean Dad? Do you hear a voice?" But before he could answer, I added, "Whose voice do you hear dad?"

"I hear a reassuring, gentle voice and, I can only imagine, but I have always believed that it is the voice of an angel," he whispered softly.

I stood there in complete awe. "Do you talk to the angel's dad?"

I then followed him out the bedroom door, and down the big flight of stairs, thinking of a dozen or more questions along the way. "But…but...how do you know...? What does an angel sound like dad?" By the time I had my last question out of my mouth, he was called to the phone and I never did get around to asking him any more questions. From that night on, I was always listening to hear a voice, a voice that my father said was an angel.

It wasn't too long after this that I could not only hear a voice, but I could see things happening that were unexplainable to everyone. I was picking up on all kinds of things about everybody. I was also pretty much convinced that I had my own personal special angel walking beside me everywhere I went, listening to my stories, giving me reassurance, and answering all my ridiculous questions. My angel talked to me like an old friend, and at any time of day or night. I could hear a soft comforting voice, feel the unexplainable energy, and see visions that I knew no one else around me could see. People were beginning to ask the question, "Who is Mary talking to?" And, quite often I would hear them answer the question with something like, "She has invisible friends," or, "She has imaginary friends."

Foreword

I didn't have to try very hard to listen for a voice any more, or be perfectly quiet like I once thought I had to be, because by this time I could be playing with a bunch of girl friends in the park, sitting at our big chaotic supper table, or in the middle of a test at school, when suddenly I would hear a voice— so clear it was like someone sitting beside me- a voice that I was becoming more and more familiar and comfortable with. It was a voice that I felt sure was my very own personal angel.

If I was about to do something that was the least bit dicey, or something that could put me in danger in any way, then the voice I heard resonated louder and deeper. If I was to go to the rescue of someone else—someone already in danger—then it was a commanding voice. If a life or death situation was about to occur, then I would instantly feel anxious—my legs would start to tremble, and I would break out in a cold sweat with a shiver up my spine. In these cases, it is much more than just listening. However I thank my dad for that advice about how to listen because if it weren't for him, I probably wouldn't have paid as much attention to listening at such an early age. I thank my mom for thinking of the bookmark that actually changed my life. It might have been old, tattered, and missing its original sheen, but the message it delivered to me at that time was like food for my soul, because I have lived by those words all my life.

Chapter 1

My First Clear Vision

I remember the time when I was 7 years old; my mother took me to a Christmas bazaar at the Catholic school I was attending—Saint Edmonds. It was a fundraiser for Girl Guides and most of the parents were there to support the cause. I still remember walking around in awe at all the colourful displays of toys, baskets, candy, fudge, flowers, knitted things, and much more, as I was hanging onto my mom's hand for dear life so as not to lose her in the crowd. I gave her a tug and pulled her towards the center of the room where there stood a baby crib complete with a beautiful doll dressed in a long white satin gown. The doll's appearance seemed angel-like to me, and I think it is what captivated me initially, beckoning me over to the center of the hall. This beautiful doll had long curly golden hair and a captivating pretty face. It was surrounded by outfits that were all hand made for her in every color of the rainbow. I was captivated by this doll from down on the floor where I was standing, at 4 feet tall. As I tried pushing my way through all the mobs of people having a look at her,

I asked my mom to lift me up so I could gain a better perspective and see everything in the crib. I remember looking at the doll from my mom's arms and saying out loud, "She looks like a baby angel." I asked mom if she could buy it for me, and of course the doll and crib were not up for sale—merely for display, as it was destined for raffle at the end of the bazaar. Well I guess I didn't know what the word raffle meant, because I just kept saying, "How will we carry her home? Can we get dad to come for her and her things?" My questions going unanswered, my mom then instructed me to print my name on the raffle ticket so I could have a chance at winning it. She handed me a pencil and a little piece of paper, and I wasted no time printing my name and phone number on it before handing it back to my mom. I watched with curiosity and excitement as she slipped my entry into the big box that was sitting upon the table beside the doll. After that, my mother had to try her hardest to pull me away from this display so I could see other attractions.

"You won't have to knit any clothes for her mom, because she already has everything she will ever need."

Mom, trying to protect me from likely disappointment, replied sympathetically, "Well you might not win it dear, so don't get too excited just yet." Then she added, "The draw is not until tomorrow at three. Suppose we wait to hear if they draw your name or not."

"They will pick my name mom, you'll see."

"I sure hope for your sake you're right dear, but don't forget—many others have their name in that box too!"

That day after we arrived home, I ran up to my room where I could hear my brothers horsing around in the room next to mine, as they usually did on any given day. By force of habit I always went into their room first to join in on the

Chapter 1 • My First Clear Vision

fun, but this particular day I remember just lying down on my bed and praying to God. I closed my eyes and visualized the doll in the crib, as I said my prayers, and instantly had a vision of the doll and the crib at the foot of my bed. I could hear a beautiful and soft voice—a voice I had never ever heard before. Remembering my dad's words, "Listen and you will hear," I listened very intently, and heard a voice clearly say, "You will have your baby doll. You will have your angel." I opened my eyes to see if anyone was in the room with me. It felt as though an angel had come to deliver me this message, and I wanted to see her with my own eyes, yet no one was there. I was disappointed simply because I wanted to ask more questions. I tried closing my eyes again, to see if I could lure any more messages, but I could not hear or see anything else, so I ran back downstairs to find my mom and dad who were sitting at the kitchen table wondering where I had got to.

When I told them of my experience of hearing a voice while I was praying, and what the voice sounded like, my dad piped up and said, "That is the voice of the Holy Spirit." I had heard my teacher Sister Louise mention the Holy Spirit many times in prayer at school, but she never ever said that we might hear the voice of the Holy Spirit. At that time, whose voice I heard didn't really matter to me; it was just *what* the voice had said that mattered most to me. When I explained that the voice said, "You will have your baby doll," they were both amused but didn't laugh. I was excited because after hearing this voice say, "You will have your baby doll," I knew it was going to be at the end of my bed just like my clear vision. That night while lying in bed, I continued to listen for the voice again, while praying out loud, but unfortunately I didn't hear anything at all. I must have kept praying until I fell asleep and when morning came, all I could think of was that it was the day that I was going to have a beautiful new doll in a crib in my room, and that it was going to be mine.

I jumped out of bed, got dressed and went about the day helping mother in the kitchen making bread and buns and even doing some dreaded homework. As the hour drew closer, I knew I was going to hear the phone ring and, I knew the voice at the other end would be one of the nuns, telling us I had won the doll. I couldn't sit still for a second, and I kept checking the clock, and the phone, to make sure no-one was on it. I told my mother and dad that they would have to go to the school to help me carry the crib and clothes—dad for the crib and mom for the clothes—since I would have my hands full with the doll. I had it all calculated out, even at seven years old! I never doubted for a minute that this angelic doll with a crib full of beautiful clothes wouldn't be beside my bed. I had such a clear vision of it that it was like it was already mine.

Shortly before three o'clock my mom was on the phone talking to my grandmother, I told her that she had to call her back later since the school would be trying to call to tell us that I'd won the raffle. She laughed and said, "Mary is expecting a phone call so we must get off the phone." They finally ended the call. The phone rang fifteen minutes later; I grabbed it and said, "Hello this is Mary."

The soft-spoken voice replied, "This is Sister Louise, at St Edmonds School—is your mother home?"

"Yes my mother is home," I cried out with excitement. I handed the phone over, giddy in anticipation.

All I remember next is my mom saying, "Yes, yes. Oh how wonderful. Well my daughter had a feeling she was going to win it—I guess she was right! Oh thank you! Thank you, very much...yes, we will come to pick it up today."

Chapter 1 • My First Clear Vision

She hung the phone up, and happily announced, "You *are* the winner, young lady! You *are* the winner! I can hardly believe it—you knew you would win this doll!" By this time both my parents were ecstatic and almost in tears, as they couldn't quite believe that I had actually predicted winning the grand prize. I said, with tears in my eyes too, "I think I will call my new doll 'Angel'." And from that day on, everywhere I went my doll Angel was in my arms—as seen in many pictures of me as a child—until the point when I outgrew dolls and relegated her to sitting upon my bed as a decoration.

Whenever the phone would ring, I would go and look for the person, no matter where they were. Even if they were out in the yard mowing the grass, or sitting in the bathtub, I would holler at them to come to the phone before anyone even answered it, because I knew who it was at the other end of the line. I would answer it with "Hello John," or "Hello Aunty Vera" and so on. This was something that happened almost every time the phone rang, and was always just laughed at by my siblings. Marginalizing the sheer improbability of my guessing consistency, they would only jokingly say, "What a coincidence, Mary knew it was you calling before we answered the phone"

Another thing I remember doing, when I was around 8 years old; I would tell my parents who was coming to visit and when the visit was going to take place. This was always a conflict of interest for me however, because I would always be questioned with, "Why didn't you tell us they phoned to say they were coming?"

I would almost get mad and say with frustration, "They didn't phone, but I just have a vision of them coming today."

Mom would always say, "What do you mean a vision?"

I would have to explain it by saying, "I just see them coming today"

Sometimes she would say, "What do you mean, you see' them"? Are you just guessing?"

"I'm not guessing mom, honest," I would say impatiently and under my breath, I would add, "You know I'm right, so why not just believe me and help me get the house ready for the company."

One time as she was helping me do the dishes, she commented, "You sure seem awfully sure of what you see"

I laughed and said, "Mom do you think I would be doing all these dirty dishes and everyone's chores if I didn't see this"? Most of the people I would see coming were relatives or friends that never ever phoned ahead of time to announce their visit, and some came very seldom throughout the year, making those predictions even more mysterious.

On another occasion, and one that my mom still talks about to this day, is when I was nine or ten years old. I had a broken arm from falling down a flight of stairs when I was horsing around on the banister, and mom asked me, "Why aren't you out playing with the other kids?"

I replied without any hesitation, "Because the house is going to be a war zone today when Leone's arrive...And I just want to put our good things away...so nothing gets broken." My mom never doubted me by this time because it seemed whenever I told them certain people were coming, they did come, and mom was always thankful I had forewarned her.

There was a time when she thought I was guessing, but after several years of continuing to be right, she would say, "Oh really. When are they coming? Do I have time to make a cake?" The first time I heard my mom ask if she had time to

Chapter 1 • My First Clear Vision

make a cake, I felt a heavy weight lifted from my shoulders because she didn't tell me any longer that it was against the Catholic religion—as I was told from the time it was evident that I could read what people were thinking, and what I was seeing in my visions.

Circumstances, times, names, places and events were proving to be right on more occasions than anyone could count or deny, And it got to be quite the normal thing around our house, that if I said someone was coming over to visit, everyone would pitch in and help tidy up, hide their precious toys that they didn't want to be played with or broken, if it was families with small children, and no one seemed to ask anymore if I was *sure* they were coming. That question had long been replaced with "*When*?"

I was eleven years old at the time. My brother Larry who was two years older than I always put my gift of intuition to the test. He would ask me questions like, "Do you see me passing my spelling test? Do you see me getting the same teacher next year? Do you see me getting caught if I play hooky? Do you see me getting the strap at school?" I answered yes to all of the above, and explained in detail that he would get caught playing hooky from school. Sure enough a few days later when Larry was late coming home after school, I knew he had to stay after class for a detention, because I could feel the strap in the palm of my hands, with a burning sensation, as though I was the one getting the strap. I could feel all day that my brother and his friend were not at school even though we all left the house together that morning. I could see him in my vision playing near water where there was a bridge. I knew they were just having fun so I didn't want to get them into trouble by telling my mom and dad—nor did I want to tell the teacher where they were if I was asked. I had it all planned out. I would say, "I never saw him," which was really a little white lie because I *had* seen him very clearly in my vision, or mind's eye. But I figured it likely they would think I was playing a trick on them, and suffer detention myself after school as well.

Unfortunately for Larry, he did get caught playing hooky after all—by Sister Louise, his favourite teacher nonetheless. The soft-spoken Sister had always liked Larry as one of her favourites, but she still had to do her job and reprimanded him accordingly for his actions. He got into trouble yet again upon arriving home, and came up to my room only to put his head in the door and say, with a long sad face, "I should have listened to you. I got the strap today *and* had to stay after school for a detention. I had to write the stupid sentence, 'I WILL NOT PLAY HOOKY EVER AGAIN' one-hundred times!"

"I'm sorry Larry," I said. "But I told you if you played hooky you would get caught."

With a sad and long face, he said, "Don't worry I've learnt my lesson". Larry went out the door in his usual jovial manner announcing, "I'm going to write the words, 'Listen to my sister,' a few times just to remind me to listen to you."

That night seemed to be an awakening for both myself and my brother. Larry said he learned always to listen to me whenever I had a vision that would prevent him from any harm. And the biggest lesson for me that night was that I actually felt someone truly believed in me and my visions. He just kept saying over and over, "I wish I would have listened to you…I wish I would have listened to you."

Later that night I was working on my arithmetic home-

Chapter 1 • *My First Clear Vision*

work in a corner of the living room while Larry was doing his homework in the dining room. I overheard him ask my mom, "How is it that only Mary see's things that we don't see"?

I smiled to myself, and said, "That's a good question, and I wonder why you don't see what I see"

"Well—" Larry said, "I guess you are just plain lucky. Can you see where my friend and I were, when we didn't go to school?" he piped up with a big laugh.

"Yes," I said laughing, "I saw you under the bridge at the creek on 6th street."

"You mean we were that obvious—that anyone could have seen us?" Larry exclaimed.

"No," I said with a smile, "I could see you as plain as day, like watching a movie. You guys were playing on the big rocks, and making a fishing rod out of a branch the way dad showed you."

"Yes you are right, that is exactly what we were doing. We wanted to see if we could catch a fish with some string, and the bologna from our sandwich. Problem was, we got caught before we could catch a fish so, we will never know if the bologna bait would have worked. I do know one thing though," Larry said, as he got up from his chair, "I'm sure lucky to have a sister like you! You'll be able to tell me if I'm going to catch a fish or not, and if I'm not, then I won't bother to go fishing. Ha, ha, ha..." he laughed, as he swung his arm out to swat me in fun.

I teased him saying, "I'm not going to tell you because you will have more fun if I don't, but I will tell you one thing for sure—you will have a better chance at catching a fish, if you use worms rather than bologna."

Chapter 2

ACCEPTING CRITICISM

Accepting any kind of criticism has always been my biggest downfall—not only as it applies in terms of being psychic, but also with other issues as I've mentioned in my first book, *Finding Happiness Without Children*. As you will see in this next story, I sometimes had to learn the hard way—how to grin and bare it, not take things so personal, and move on...

I remember one occasion; it was my 16th birthday. I was thrown a surprise birthday party at a friend's home where a few of the girls presented me with gifts of candy, elegant stationary and other little keepsakes that I felt honoured to receive. One of the girls suggested reading the cards aloud and passing them around for everyone to see. The words inside one of the cards were written by one of the girls named Beverly who—a clown at the best of times—was always trying to make people laugh. Her words however were ones that not only embarrassed me, but made me feel strange, different, annoyed and upset. They were words that I had never before heard describing me. In fact, they were words that I couldn't accept or forget. They were scribed in crimson red ink—"To Mary, my friend that seems to be a WITCH." I was noticeably dismayed, agitated even. Furthermore, I hadn't read aloud, which of course made everyone more curious as to what the inside of the card said.

My feelings were hurt so deeply from that one word "witch" and I couldn't quite seem to get past it. I talked about it with all my other friends that were there that night, and they all said more or less the same thing, "She didn't mean it." And even though it might have been said as a joke, I found myself unable to just let it go and forget about it. We didn't see much of each other after this particular incidence until a few years later, when I had a very strong feeling about her. I kept thinking about her all the time, and one night while I was lying in bed, I heard the voice. Only this time it was like an order or a command—"Get in touch with Beverly. She is ill, she needs you." My heart skipped a beat, as I shot up from my bed with a vision of her in a white gown in a hospital bed. Not realizing it was 1 in the morning; I got dressed and was ready to shoot out the door when I heard the voice come to me again saying, "Not now, tomorrow, tomorrow." I turned around, took my coat off, and went back to bed. Lying there all night, wide awake, knowing that something was terribly wrong with my friend, made me feel sick to my stomach, and I couldn't help but think that I had let our friendship drift away simply because of a stupid word.

As soon as daylight dawned, I was up writing in my diary about how foolish I was to almost lose a friend over the fact that she had once called me a name I didn't like. I decided that I wouldn't go in to the salon I was working at after school; I would go to her work place at the *A&W* instead.—to confirm what my feelings and perceptions were.

As I sat on the rolling bus I had a clear vision of her in the white gown lying in a hospital bed, but I continued to head for her place of work just the same. The bus-stop was directly in front of the *A&W* and I exited my ride in great haste from the middle-doors. As soon as I stepped foot upon the sidewalk, I felt for sure Beverly was not there. I went inside and quickly looked around. I could see two car-hop girls scurrying about, and I asked one of them, "Do you know when Beverly is working?" I could tell by the look on their face that they didn't quite know how to answer. One of the girls replied in a rather sad tone, "Beverly isn't working right now...actually, she's in the hospital."

"Thanks," I said, as I pushed open the heavy glass door. I knew that I had to catch the next bus to the hospital, so that I could see my friend Bev.

I arrived, out of breath and feeling sick to my stomach. I told the nurses I was a sister from out of town so that I could go in before visiting hours—a little white-lie that I would ask God's forgiveness for later, as all I wanted to do was to go and see my friend Beverly, and tell her how sorry I was that she was sick, and to let her know that I felt badly for being mad at her. As I walked down the sterile white hallway I was kind of in a daze but glancing into the rooms as I walked by them. I looked in at a lady who appeared to be about 75 years old. She was lying down and facing the door. I remember thinking how sad it was to see such a frail looking lady. I proceeded down the corridor until I knew I had gone too far and ended up back by the same room I had just peered into. I went inside and I looked around, glancing at the patients on either side. None looked familiar. It was then that I heard the voice from the bed where I had just seen the frail little lady. She called my name very softly, "Mary, hi."

Chapter 2 • Accepting Criticism

I turned and went over to her bed. I wrapped my arms around her and said, "Beverly how are you?"

With tears she gripped both my hands and said, "Well I have bowel Cancer and that is why I've lost so much weight." I took a deep breath before I knew what to say next. "Sit here on the bed," she said with a slight smile as she pulled me down to the side of the bed where we held hands and talked, just like old times.

The conversation I was dreading came up of course and when Beverly said, "I know I shouldn't have written those mocking words on your birthday card...I'm so sorry that I did. I need you to forgive me, because you have always been my friend and I love you."

As her words came, tears were streaming down both our faces. I said, "Beverly, just know one thing. I am the one who was stubborn and unforgiving...I am the one who should be asking for forgiveness, not you!" I wouldn't care if you called me a witch, or any other name," I replied. "I'm just happy that I can be here right now, and that we can talk and enjoy this time together."

With tired sad eyes, and hands that could hardly squeeze mine in her grip, Beverly continued in a soft and serious tone, "I know now that you really do have a talent for seeing things that other people don't, and I just didn't know anything about it when I called you a witch. But since then," she said with tears welling up again in her eyes, "I have come to realize that people who can see things before they happen are called psychic. I had never before heard those words or I would have called you that instead of..."

"Hush, hush," I said, as I gently grasped her small frail hand one more time.

She smiled and told me, "I know one thing...I should have said in your card; 'To my friend who seems to be an angel. I believe you really are one."

My dear friend passed away only a few years later, and I was very distraught with her departure. I kept thinking that had I been able to accept criticism a little better, I would not have lost those years of friendship with a good friend, whose life was cut so short. One night, not long after her passing, she appeared at the foot of my bed. She was happy and looked vibrant and healthy. I asked her once again to forgive me for my faults or stress I may have caused her when we were growing up. She smiled and replied in a serene and soft voice, "I've got much more important things to think about now." I returned her smile and reached out to touch her but, before I could reach her, she was no longer there. I have seen her face in the clouds several times, and I often hear her laughing voice. On many occasions, right out of the blue, I have heard her saying, "How're you doing, you little witch!" Every time, I laugh to myself and look around to see if she is there. It gives me an incalculable sense of calm to know she is right beside me in spirit.

Beverly taught me several indelible lessons from that single experience. One of them was to swallow my pride, and forgive people for any wrong doings because it can very easily be too late, too soon. The other lesson was to always trust your instincts and your intuition—the voice we all hear from time to time and too often never follow up on! May you always rest in peace Beverly!

On another occasion, before I knew all the names that psychics inevitably would get called at some time or another was once when I was in the middle of a reading for a friend of my brothers whom I had never read before. I was quite taken aback and every time I would pick up on

Chapter 2 • Accepting Criticism

something that was bang-on, she would repetitively utter, "That is too weird," or, "You're making me scared." These phrases were redundantly repeated and all the while she would be writing down every word—names, dates, and scenarios that were relevant to her life. Her summation was, "This is too scary for me...too crazy—you're spooking me out."

It wasn't until many years later that I realized what these people really meant to say is that *we* are "unbelievable"— not the reading! The readings are always accurate when they have these words to say, or they wouldn't be saying it. I had a hard time getting used to the these phrases.

I had always thought of psychics as special, gifted, amazing—or just plain incredible. I had a hard time when anyone called me 'weird' or 'wacky.' Yes, we *are* different alright—because we see visions, hear voices, and act on our impulses. We can read peoples' soul path. But what most don't know, is that we psychics are here to help people find their 'camino'—or 'way'—in life, and ultimately, their true purpose. The interesting thing is, that everyone has intuition, instinct, premonition, but most people don't want it, or don't know they have it, so therefore don't practice it.

How often do you hear people say; "I had a bad feeling about that person the first time I seen him/her" and in the end after finding out that they were right, they then say:"I should have listened to my feelings that I had"

As time went on and people came to me after a reading and went on and on about how much I had helped and guided them through their very difficult time—or guided them to their life purpose—I wasn't bothered nearly as much by the sometimes derogatory comments and negative labels.

Another time when I was hurt and confused was when

I was just starting out as a reader in the early '70s. A friend—or who I once thought was a friend—had me over for a cup of tea and quickly directed the conversation towards the psychic realm. She told me in a forthright manner, "My husband and your husband work together. I understand you read people." I knew where this was going, but I hadn't been confronted with someone face to face on the subject before. I felt my heart starting to race with indignation. My face began to flush. Before I could say a word, she pre-empted me with, "Did you know that what you're doing is a *cult*?"

My eyebrows rose, as I replied, "What do you mean, a *cult*?" not really wanting to hear her answer.

"Don't you know what a cult is?" she snapped with disgust. "It is the work of the Devil. And, also," she continued, as I was handed a pocketbook that was conveniently sitting upon her counter top, "it is very evil! You need to read this book that is all about the cult and you will want to stop doing your psychic readings when you get finished with it."

"I'm sorry to tell you," I began to say, "but my work as a reader is no different from that of a psychologist, only I don't go by any books—I go by the messages I receive from a higher energy source." Actually, at the time, saying this sounded good since I didn't really know a whole lot about what I was talking about but it nonetheless came effortlessly out of my mouth from somewhere. I remember glancing at the book and purposely not opening the cover. I put it down in the center of her table, as if to say, I'm not interested. I then attempted to instil some enlightenment, although not with a whole lot of expectation. "Well I happen to know that what I have is a special gift from God, and it has *nothing* to do with the Devil. It has however, *everything* to do with our soul."

"And who told you that?" she inquired with an arrogant

snort.

"My heart, my soul, and my inner-voice." I said, before she could ask further questions or make another statement. Making for a quick exit and halfway to the door I said with plain simplicity, "I'm not here to convert your beliefs or make you a believer in God's gifts." As I was turning the door knob to make my way out, saying goodbye and thanking her for the tea, she insisted on tucking the little book into my jacket pocket! I knew in my heart that this was the last time I would be seeing this narrow-minded, self-styled lecturer. Once I had finally got out the door I noticed a black mailbox attached to her railing. As I walked down the steps I lifted the lid and—with a serene sense of satisfaction—slipped the pocket book into it.

I told my husband what had happened that day. He simply said, "You will come across many people in your life that won't approve of the things you do. So, you have to stay strong. You have to stay focused and continue doing your gifted work as a psychic, and believe in yourself as you always have."

From that day on, I knew I was going to continue on with my readings as usual. I had the tenacity and the fortitude to rise above such negativity. Nothing would change my mind or get me confused. I knew I was doing the right thing—it was what I felt in my bones, my heart and every cell in my body! I was always told that it is a gift that I have, not anything to do with a cult, and that was good enough for me. That night I lay in bed thanking God for the strength he gave me to stand up for what I believed, and also for not letting her harsh and hurtful words and accusations change my mind or doubt myself. Before I fell asleep, I felt as though a heavy burden was lifted from my shoulders and my heart, just knowing that I had finally learned how to deal with the criticism and negativity. This made me feel really good and, luckily for me, the sensation endures to this day. I felt for sure that what I said were the words given to me by spirit or angel, because I didn't quite know what I was saying—or what it exactly meant—but I did know that what I believed in was what I wanted to do all my life. I quietly thanked both God and my dear angel, and as I was doing so, I could make out a faint and fading, "Time to go to sleep, it's way past your bedtime."

Chapter 3

Ouija Boards

When I was growing up, everything and anything that was the least bit paranormal was a taboo—not just because we were of strong Catholic background—but because we were from 'old-school' conservative thinking. Many believed such things would bring bad luck to the person or, to the family. Of course for us kids, the curiosity was compounded by the fact that it was a 'no-no.' I was quite fascinated with the new little board game called 'Ouija' when it was introduced to me one day at a friend's house. A few of us adventurous girls were more intrigued than anything, and I for one wanted to know just exactly how it worked. Summing it up in my own mind, it became very clear to me that it was something to do with a person's energy. Everyone has different energy intensities, so naturally it would work differently for everyone who played it. That particular night we almost wore the thing out playing it for hours and hours at a time. I wanted to take it home with me but I instinctively knew that it would be thrown out as soon as it was discovered what it was all about. The only alternative was going to my friend's house to play on it. Even there, we had to hide it under her bed so that no one would inadvertently discover it. Since my friend was also Italian Catholic, her parents—like mine—would not want us playing with anything they thought to be evil or considered a potential contagion of bad luck. It was one thing that they knew I had a built-in sensor as to who was phoning or coming to visit, but to play on a board that had an evil stigma attached to it would be going beyond pushing my luck.

On one occasion, a 14th birthday party, I was staying overnight at a friend's house along with a few other girls when someone gave a Ouija board as a gift. This didn't come as a big surprise to any of us, as it was all she talked about for weeks prior to her birthday. Everyone, of course, wanted their turn to ask it questions, and each one of us sat around in fascination as the flurry of queries began. Our mouths dropped open on many occasions as some of the uncanny things that transpired that night were extraordinary *and* scary. There was a feeling we got that convinced us to play longer—it seemed to want us to ask even more questions. We were up half the night playing on this mesmerizing board. One of the girls asked, "Why is it called 'Ouija board'? What does Ouija mean? Who invented it? Is it a *bad thing*? Will bad things happen to us if we keep playing with it?" These were just a few of the questions that would typically come up every time we played the board.

That night we decided that we no longer liked the name 'Ouija.' It didn't sound like a nice enough name for something we wanted to spend so much of our time playing with. So we made up a little fun game of our own, which was to see who could come up with the best name for our esoteric Ouija board. We all had to write down an individually chosen secret name on a little piece of paper. Then, without telling anyone what we had written, we had to fold it up, and put it in an empty popcorn bowl. At the end of the night we were to shake it up and draw only one name out, read it out loud, and toss it back into the bowl.

Chapter 3 • Ouija Boards

Whatever name was first to appear three times would be the name we would give to our Ouija board. We all knew by this time that there really was energy attached to it, and the more we used it, the more we wanted to continue investigating its potential.

At 11 o'clock the seven of us girls gathered around in a circle, ready to draw the names. For some reason I was elected to start us off. I gave the bowl a brisk shake up, pulled out the first name and unfolded the scrap of paper. It read 'Spirit Board.' Hmmm, we all said in unison, not knowing who had selected this particular name. Then Joanne pulled a name and read aloud, "Angel board!"

"I like that name," a few of us whispered. The third name, pulled by Gail, was 'Magic Board.' This went on for another round until the name 'Spirit Board' came up twice more. This seemed more than appropriate since the name was selected by none other than the birthday-girl herself! From that day on, the crazy board became our fun and our game of choice and we always called it our 'Spirit Board.'

One particular night the same bunch of us girls got permission to have a sleep-over at our friend Sylvia's. This was not a common occurrence for sure, but since it was a birthday party, we received 'official' clearance. We enjoyed games, prizes, birthday cake and of coarse our special 'Spirit Board.' We all sat around in a circle on the floor asking it questions that no one else knew about. Before long we heard Sylvia's mom yelling to us from the background, saying it was an evil thing, and that we were not allowed to use it any more. She made it clear in no uncertain terms that it was not welcome in her house.

"Why mom?" Sylvia asked, dejectedly.

"Because it is an evil entity that might bring bad luck to our family and home," her mom asserted, in a voice that meant 'do as I say, and don't ask any questions!' Our party wasn't completely crashed by the wave of disappointment that washed over us, because our desire and determination to play with the Spirit Board was greater than mere harsh words.

That night we crawled into our makeshift beds, still dismayed over the ruling. We were close to falling asleep when we heard a hopeful voice whispering from underneath the blankets, "I have a good idea, why don't you bring it to my house one night. My mom won't know exactly what it is and we can ask it all the questions we want!"

We realized the whispered voice was from our new found friend who had recently arrived from Italy. "Are you sure you want to do this Connie?" someone asked excitedly.

"Yes, I'm sure. My mom and dad are likely not to mind."

"Okay. Let's put the Spirit Board into a bag and carry it over to your house after school one day," I said with optimism.

"It will look like part of our homework from school!" Connie added.

"But what if it really is cursed by the devil like so many people say it is. Maybe something bad could happen to us!" I suggested.

"Yah, you're right. Maybe we'd better throw it in the garbage and forget we ever saw it," Connie said, with undisguised sarcasm.

"You could be right." I said, "We are suppose to be good Catholics— Maybe we shouldn't be playing with such things." After thinking it over we all more or less agreed. "Okay, but before we sentence it to exile, what harm could there be in asking it just one last little question?" I suggest-

Chapter 3 • Ouija Boards

ed. Seeking a majority agreement, I asked, "Is everyone okay with this?" A unanimous approval was reached. It was plainly obvious to us all that we were looking forward to seeing what the next encounter would bring.

We went to school the following Monday and I found I couldn't get to Connie's house fast enough once classes had ended. Only problem was, three of the other girls were unable to go. Luckily my mom had said it would be okay for a half hour, but no more—all the time I needed to ask the question I so wanted to know! We marched into her house with our school books and lunch kits all the while assuming our usual nonchalance. Nothing looked suspicious or amiss as we had stuffed the Spirit Board inside Connie's coat and wrapped it up like it was a pile of books. We then swiftly made our way to her bedroom up on the second floor. Everyone drew a sigh of relief, knowing that we could have very easily got caught along the way.

We were readying ourselves upon the floor with our question in hand when Connie's mom burst into the room with a broom in her hands as if ready to sweep the floor. With a sweet and gentle smile, that seemed to say, "Ah ha! I caught you!" She came closer to have a better look at what we were up to. With her three fingers pinched together in front of our face, the way most Italians do when they express themselves—especially when emotional—she inquired with a suspicious tone in her deep voice, "Ki Fi?" or, 'What are you doing?' in English.

We gulped, wondering what Connie would say. "Mom it's nothing." Unfortunately, her mom was not walking away—in fact she appeared to be fascinated by this little, odd looking board. She actually asked us to continue playing because she wanted to see what exactly it was we were doing. We couldn't lie and were left with no choice but to try and explain the concept to her. Connie gave it her best shot, "You just ask a question while resting your fingers very lightly upon the little piece of wood, then it moves around the board" As the question is being asked, the little board starts to move, and it goes to the letters with the energy in your fingers, spelling out the answer to the question."

As this was all being said in Italian, I could only study the look on Connie's mom's face to determine her reaction. She said something else and Connie promptly translated for me. "My mother is saying if the board is what you say it is she wants to ask it one of her own questions that none of you know the answer to." Without hesitation, we all quickly agreed. I'm sure all of our heads were thinking the same thing—that if she believes in it we would be able to play with our Spirit Board any old time we wanted to and, in the privacy of at least one of our homes.

Connie's mom pulled up a chair as if to settle in for the night, and said without another thought, or even a question, "Ask it for the name of my cousin who is sick in Italy." She exhaled in Italian dialect. Louisa and I who were at the command of the little board, while it started to move, finding letters that we were too nervous to read, and as it moved back and forth, and back and forth again. It spelled out the word 'Teresa.' It was obvious to us that the correct—and rapid—answer had startled Connie's mom, as much as it surprised us. Her mom went hysterical and wasted no time ordering us to take it out of the house immediately. Agitated, she walked out of the room, and we knew we wouldn't have much time at our disposal to ask the questions we were so patiently waiting to ask.

I wanted to go first since I had only a half hour before going home. So I sat and I asked, "Please tell me what I am

Chapter 3 • Ouija Boards

going to do in my life." Incredibly the little board spelled out the words, "help"

"What does that mean?" Connie pondered.

"I don't know exactly. Let's ask the question again—just to see if it says the same thing. I tested the board again with the same question but slightly altered, "What am I going to do in my life for work?" It spelled out the word "gift." Connie interpreted the reply with enthusiasm,

"You're getting a gift"

I shook my head and said, "I have to go now." Picking up my coat and books, I went out the door bidding, "goodbye and see you tomorrow." Making my way down the porch and onto the walkway I was talking to myself, "I don't know what "gift" I would be getting—my birthday is a long ways off, and so is Christmas!"And what does "Help" mean?

All the bad rap that the Ouija board had during that era and as much as we realized it had a sometimes startling and alarming feel to it, it was never enough to stop us from playing with our Spirit Board. As a matter of fact we were even more intrigued with it as the years went by. A few of us girls, well into our early twenties and thirties, would get together every once in awhile to have a 'Spirit Board Night.' We would typically bring pot-luck snacks and sandwiches, stories, and of course lots of well thought out questions to ask our Spirit Board.

One particular evening we thought to ask it a question about someone who had passed away. When we wondered who we should inquire about, the name Mario came out of the blue. Mario was Maria's late husband. He was taken from her very suddenly due to a heart attack. Naturally, we all thought it would be nice to make contact with him if we could. Maria sat down with me at the Spirit Board ready to ask him a question. When the little board started to move we knew it was a good sign. The letters began to spell out the words, "be happy...sell house...move on." This confirmed to us once again that the Spirit Board indeed is an energy field that seems to be guided by spirits or angels. We all had a tear in our eye by this time, and felt the distinct presence of Mario in the room with us, smiling and sitting right beside us. It wasn't long after this incident, that Maria put the house up for sale—even though it held all of her happiest memories—sold it, and was able to move on with her life. People will still say that the Ouija board is unnerving, even frightening, and shouldn't be fooled with. I still feel however that it has a sacred feel to it, and should be respected. As for the words "Gift and "Help that were spelled out on the ouigi board for me, I made up my own interpretation of what they meant many years later when I started reading professionally. I felt the word "Gift" was my Gift of intuition"

Chapter 4

FINDING MY TRUE PURPOSE

Years later, when most of us girls went our own separate ways, got married and found careers that took us to other parts of the country, some of our group simply didn't keep in touch. They drifted away, never to be heard from again. Some however—as few as they may be—didn't leave, and are still living in the same place today. It seemed the ones that didn't take psychic readers or paranormal serious, were the ones we never heard from again. The ones fascinated—or at least curious—about the metaphysical world are the ones that to this day are not only still very closely connected to one another, but are also still connected to the metaphysical world. They are seasoned spiritual counsellors and in fact are well known psychic individuals.

I, for one, was always curious about what a reader could tell me, as I could never seem to predict my own life path. At a very young age I found myself always at the mercy of card readers, psychics, tea-cup readers, anywhere and everywhere just to give me some guidance and confirmation as to whether or not being an intuitive reader was really all I was meant to do, since it came to me so easy, I wondered if there was more to it. And even after many readers telling me that one day I would be sitting in their seat, reading people from all walks of life and from all parts of the world, I still seemed to need confirmation. Until one night just after saying my prayers in bed before falling asleep, I heard a voice say, "If things are meant to be, they will be. If you are meant to read intuitively, you will. Now go to sleep—its way past your bedtime." I believe that we all get little omens that seem to come face-to-face with us when we are searching for answers, and that they are definitely signals to pay attention to. I feel they are like our angels and spirit guides trying to help us get to where we are suppose to be.

This very thing happened to me one day as I was trying to find a place to park on my way to the bank. I went around the block several times, getting more tired and frustrated by the minute in the heat and busy traffic. Finally, I found a spot under a towering shade tree. How nice I thought to myself—maybe this is going to be a good day after all! While I was walking towards the bank I passed by a lovely little consignment shop that had balloons and signs everywhere announcing "GRAND OPENING." There was clothing, clocks, books, china, and small pieces of furniture. It all looked as though it had been hand-picked and sorted through, with a fine tooth comb, ensuring a high standard of quality for what was selected.

"What a lovely little boutique you have," I commented after taking all this in. I wandered throughout the shop in a leisurely fashion with nothing in particular catching my eye until I walked past a bookcase that was titled "SELF HELP." The letters were so big that I thought even someone visually impaired would notice it. I found myself skimming through the titles as if I was looking for my own book. I've read so many of these kinds of books I thought to myself, that 'Self Help' should be my middle name. I was skim-

Chapter 4 • Finding My True Purpose

ming over all the familiar names like Louise Hay, Barbara De Angelis, and Fran Hewitt when suddenly I came across a book that looked familiar. It was a book I'd read several times by Louise Hay, called *You Can Heal Your Life*. I was about to put it back upon the shelf, when I heard a little voice whisper in my ear, "Hang onto this book." The peculiar thing was I still had a copy at home, in my own bookcase. So, why would I buy another one? Why was I drawn to this particular book anyway? "I get it," I said to myself, there *is* a message in it that I have to find. I found myself gripping this little book that seemed to feel warm to the touch. I held it tightly in my hands and began flipping through its pages. It was as though I was looking for something I had lost. It was very strange and I felt there had to be a good reason why I was in this particular shop in the first place, especially when I was supposed to be going to the bank. As I was flipping through the pages of this very familiar little book, I noticed a tiny piece of paper fall free and onto the floor. When I reached down for it, it seemed to be nothing more than just a blank piece of faded yellow paper. I turned it over and squinted to see the scribble of a few faint words which read; "Psychic Reader, Norma Johnson, Salmon Arm." Hmm, I was thinking to myself. This, I was sure, was the reason I came into this shop, not to really buy anything, not even for this book. It was only for the name of this psychic lady. This was another one of those little omens that seem to touch us on the shoulder and send shivers up our spine.

All I could think of at that moment was, *This is an omen, and who is she?*

"Can I help you?" a soft voice from behind the counter asked.

"Oh no, thank you."

"Did you find everything you were looking for? she then asked.

"Oh yes, thanks," I said cheerfully with a smile,

"I've found exactly what I was looking for." I paid for the book and left the store with more than just the book in hand for someone whom I felt was going to enjoy it as much as I did but, more importantly, I sensed as though I had the name of someone who had an important message for me.

Yes, I know how ridiculous it sounds but, to me at the time, it felt almost miraculous. I tucked the little piece of paper away in my wallet as if it was the map to a lost treasure, and as soon as I got in my front door, and kicked off my shoes, I grabbed the phone book down off the shelf, to see if I could find the number and address for this Norma Johnson. I quickly opened the phone book as I normally would, and was stunned to see that the book—as big as it was—had opened to the exact page that the Johnson name was on! My focus zoomed in on the very name I was looking for as well. *What are the odds of that?* I pondered, as I wrote out the number. I was more than amazed, I was astonished. I kept saying out loud, "This is definitely another omen." Five hundred pages of listings and the book literally opened to the very page I needed to find this unknown woman. I had the feeling that she was elderly and that she loved flowers, I was picking up that she was surrounded with beautiful friends, family and gardens.

The voice at the other end of the phone sounded soft, gentle, and a bit tired and elderly. "Hello, Mrs Johnson speaking"

"Hi, I was wondering if I could make an appointment for a reading"

Chapter 4 • Finding My True Purpose

"Certainly...how does tomorrow afternoon at 2:00 sound"?

"Perfect, was my only reply, as I was still in awe over the phone-book incident.

"What's your address Mrs Johnson?" I asked as I reached for a pen.

With what Norma had told me for directions, I had sketched a map in my mind and I figured I could remember the way by mere visualization and landmarks. When the time came to venture out and find my way to this appointment, I quickly realized that I didn't know where anything was located in this idyllic little community. So I just set out thinking that sooner or later I would reach the right house by way of energy and some of the landmarks she gave me. I found myself driving all around the beautiful little town, not recognizing a single thing. After a half hour of being completely lost, and driving all around the town over and over again, I heard a comforting little voice inside my head saying, "Get turned around, your going the wrong way." And at that, I swung the car around, making an attempt at a U-turn on the narrow rocky road when I became aware of a very peculiar sensation. It was at that moment that I felt as though someone else was driving the car! Nothing around me was familiar except the corner gas station and grocery store that I had stopped at many years before. Again my steering wheel seemed to automatically want to make another turn, this time to the left and, amused, I looked out the passenger window and caught a glimpse of what I knew was the right house. It was a tiny bungalow that was like something out of a storybook. Colourful flowers peered out from gingerbread looking window-boxes. Patio ornaments and fountains were featured throughout what appeared to be a perfectly manicured yard. I slowly made my way up to the orange-red painted door, admiring and smelling the fragrances of the wonderful array of flowers all along the walkway. *The flowers are a reflection of her soul,* I thought.

I lifted the big heavy brass door-knocker and let it go, turning one last time to get another whiff of the expanse of aromatic flowers just as the door opened. A small-framed and fragile looking elderly woman with the softest voice said, "You must be Mary. Do come in dear," she said, as she held out her hand with a warm and comforting smile. From the foyer, she walked me down a brightly decorated hallway to her reading room. "I feel you will be changing your name," she said matter-of-factly, as she pulled out a comfy padded red armchair and gestured for me to sit.

The room looked like a greenhouse with light filtering through the glass windows that housed hibiscus and a variety of palm trees. Looking about the room, I could see that she had a special interest in sacred stones, statues, feathers, books, candles and cards. I was busy looking at the stones when she said out of the blue, "Who is Steve?"

"Steve is my husband," I said with my jaw half-dropped. *Wow!* I began thinking. I'd hardly sat down and she was already aware of my husband's name, and that I was planning on changing my first name. Even more bewildering since this was coming from someone I had never before met. I had an inkling as to what was coming next, and I was totally ready to hear anything she would pick up. I wanted to hear it from someone else if only to confirm my own feelings.

Sitting directly across from me, and eyeing me up from head to toe, I was wishing I had brought my tape recorder. "You already know what I am going to tell you, but I will tell you anyway," she said as she began shuffling the cards.

Chapter 4 • *Finding My True Purpose*

"You have lost yourself along the way, and through the shuffle you have lost your spirit too. You will find yourself again when you are no longer with your present husband. You have grown yes, but you will evolve to your higher self—your spiritual self. Do you understand?" she asked, looking me straight in the eyes over her heavy rimmed bifocals. "Does this make sense to you dear?" Looking directly back at her gaze, I noticed that she seemed to be in some kind of a trance. She continued to shuffle the cards.

"Yes, it certainly does make a lot of sense, only, where is my direction going to take me?" was my response. "I need to know *where* I am heading," I added with a slight note of hesitation.

"You are heading into a new adventurous era; it's filled with light and hope. You have been in the dark for so long dear. Now you will find your spirit that you have lost along the course of your journey—your soul and your mind will merge together as one. What is coming your way will change your life. The spirit and holiness of the Creator will fill you and you will find your soul purpose. You were born with a supernatural gift you see, and it's important that you share your gift with the world."

Slouched in my chair and feeling as though this woman already owned my soul, I took a deep breath and replied, "I'm hearing you loud and clear Norma." She reached out and squeezed my hand and closed her eyes.

"You need not be afraid of change. Your life will take on a new meaning when you find your Soul Purpose." When you find your soul and your spirit, you will help others do the same. Is this making any sense to you dear?"

I found myself trying to absorb the entirety of all she was telling me. Taking another deep breath and with my eyes starting to well-up, I announced, "Well Mrs Johnson, it makes more sense to me than you would likely think!" She handed me the box of tissues that sat beside her on a side table.

"Don't worry," she said encouragingly. "In fact," she continued, with a big smile and a little wink, "Your purpose in life is to share your gift of intuition and be an inspiration to others." I gave her a hug and thanked her for her kind words, and as she walked me to the door, she said some parting words that I have never since forgotten. "You have a God given gift', and you need to share it with the world, you need to help people, guide them, but you must first believe in yourself.

"Thank you, thank you," I said, as I chocked back some tears.

The reading was over before I knew it, or so it seemed. I have no recollection as to how long the reading was, or even how much I paid. All I remember is that this woman changed my life forever. She had faith in me and I had trust in her.

As I walked along her beautiful walkway to the little white picket gate, and feeling as though she was still watching me, and wanted to say something more, I turned to wave a final goodbye, and sure enough- the words still ring in my ears today, "Don't worry my dear, you will not be lost for long. You will fit all the pieces of the puzzle together, and when you do, your world will open up before your very eyes. You will become the woman who you were always meant to be."

The intoxicating scent of lavender bushes—a flurry of purple and white blossoms swaying gently in the breeze—combined with the subtle aroma of alyssum that appeared to command her entire walkway. "Thank you for having such faith in me" I said as I waved goodbye and disap-

Chapter 4 • Finding My True Purpose

peared around the corner of her house. Her words were still filtering through my head all the way home and into the night; *Lost, name change, inspiration, spirit, born with a gift, believe in myself, my soul purpose.* It was just then I remembered getting lost trying to find her house. I began thinking to myself. *Maybe that was what she meant by 'the Spirit'. Maybe it was my spirit-guide that had escorted me to her house.* I never wrote any of her reading down, simply because I was so mesmerized by her and what she was telling me—especially the way she was so sure that I had lost my way, but that I would find my soul purpose. This I found amazing, intriguing, and encouraging. As I drove home I felt as though I was in a whole new wonderful world, one that I wanted to share with everyone. I remember thinking that she was the second psychic reader that picked up that my name would change, only I forgot to ask her what my name was going to be...

This psychic reader made me realize that I might have been lost, but that I was really on the right path all along, only I didn't know it. I no longer wondered where I was suppose to be, what I was suppose to be doing or, if I was doing the right thing. Norma Johnson had answered all those questions for me that day. When I arrived home that day I kept thinking of all the things she not only confirmed for me, and envisioned for my future, but the things that I had been blocking out for years were suddenly brought to light. One of her most valuable insights was that my marriage really was over. Her analysis was in fact correct—my husband and I really were on two different planes going in opposite directions. This statement alone seemed to keep ringing in my ears until the day my husband of twenty-five years and I went to the lawyer's office filing for a legal separation. I realized that if it wasn't for Mrs Johnson, I would probably have never taken the time to sit back and analyze the true facts of my relationship even though deep in my heart, I knew—and felt—it really was over. It took her inspiring words to convince me to take those giant steps on my own. Her words were infectious. Her reading changed the way I looked at myself, my life, my name, other people and my gifts.

From that day on, I never, ever looked back. I continued to be a confident intuitive, with a passion to help others reach their goals, connect with their higher self, and find their soul purpose as I did. I also made a solemn oath to myself, that if I wanted to change my name, I didn't need approval from anyone, as long as I was happy with the name change.

Chapter 5

PSYCHIC EXPECTATIONS

"Never look down to test the ground before taking your next step, only he who keeps his eye fixed on the far horizon will find the right road."

~Dag Hammarskjold

After my reading from Mrs Johnson, I knew that my real happiness was within my soul. It resided in my ability of being able to help people from all walks of life. I felt that God gave me this gift to share—to help people—so why would I want to abandon or marginalize it, or not use it to help those who needed it.

So, it began, or should I say, *I* began, to study up on all the paranormal information I could get my hands on. And realized that I was not alone in feeling the way I did about labels and expectations, in fact it was becoming quite evident that most psychics are perceived as possessing "special powers," not "gifts." but Because of this "power" label, many are often alienated from family and/or the 'normal crowd.' But really, if those people would only realize that we are all born with a third eye—the spiritual eye—whereby we can see much more than we are typically aware. This is the intuitive consciousness eye. If everyone trusted their own instincts, and believed in the higher self, and listened to their energy field (which we are all made up of), they would then act upon the information they heard. Unfortunately, only a small percentage of us live by this knowledge while the biggest percentage does not. Relative to the majority, we are considered the strange or abnormal ones, because of the uncanny, unexplainable experiences that our educated eye can see.

In the book by "Larry Dossey' called, "The power of Premonition" he gives us another explanation of intuition and precognition. He says the mind is nonlocal" and though it is lodged in the brain, and locked inside the skull, it has the ability to sweep out beyond time and space to grasp at everything and everywhere.

We have always believed that time moves forward just like a clock, but in theory, Dossey notes that time can move in any direction. That time can move forward, sideways and backwards, and can expose all information to the infinite mind. The unhindered power of the nonlocal mind.

After forty-some odd years of delving into peoples' souls, and having people ask "How do you just know" or "How can you just see it" Dossey's explanation seems to answer both those questions. It certainly gave me a new perspective on Intuition.

Chapter 6

THE ULTIMATE LESSON

I remember when there was a time I doubted even my own messages. I would hear a message, loud and clear, while reading a client, and wonder what it meant. Sometimes it didn't make much sense. In fact it was often that it didn't make any sense whatsoever to me. I would hesitate, and not necessarily want to tell my client what I was picking up simply because I couldn't at the time see a correlation. I would try blocking it out, but the word or words would just fly out of my mouth anyway, as funny as this sounded. It took a few clients coming back and telling me word for word of ridiculous or bizarre incidents when I began to realize that I am not able to understand *every-thing* I hear or see. And that's okay...

I learned the 'ultimate lesson' when I first started reading as a professional in the '70s. I was hairdressing in a little salon in Lynn Valley—a small community in North Vancouver, British Columbia. A very attractive looking young German woman walked in from the street and asked if she could have a reading right then and there. She was a bit loud, and with heavy accent, but very polished and business like. Even though I was finished for the day and looking forward to getting home and putting my tired feet up with a cup of tea in hand, I decided to accept this young and somewhat mysterious woman's request. She seemed a bit desperate. It didn't take me long to realize she was seeking some answers to some troubling questions.

She introduced herself as Greta. I could sense by her anxious demeanor that she was in what could only be called 'a state of disarrayed hurry.' She didn't want to waste any time chatting about the weather. I dispatched her expensive looking coat and managed to get her sitting comfortably in one of the chairs. While she was rummaging in her oversized purse for something, I point-blank asked her, "Who is Marc?"

Not looking up, and still tossing things about in her purse she replied with a snort, "Dat ease my son. Vhere do you see him?"

Smiling, laying out the cards, I told her, "I see the spelling different. There is a 'C' at the end of his name rather than a 'K.'"

"Yaw, das is true."

It was not surprising to me that I had picked up his name since I could tell by the sparkle in her eye that the sun rose and shone around this son of hers. Basically, that is all she wanted to talk about and so we did. We ended the reading an hour later with Greta quite excited with what I had told her. I had seen her son Marc moving from Germany to live in Canada, helping her build the house of her dreams. The reading itself didn't seem to be any different than any other. As for picking up her son's name, I didn't think too much about it, because very often names will come through instantly for me. They are clear and strong and, are almost always a child, family member, relative or friend. Many times it can be someone close to them that has passed over to the other side. A funny thing happened

Chapter 6 • The Ultimate Lesson

however this particular time, and it also happened the following morning, during my first reading for a woman in her mid-forties who was visiting the Vancouver area and, who coincidently was also from Germany.

I kept picking up the same name for her as the lady from Germany twenty-four hours earlier. I wondered why this name was still surfacing in this unrelated reading. The name I kept getting was once again Marc, spelt with a 'C' instead of a 'K.' I remember thinking to myself, *why is this name still buzzing around? Why am I still seeing the word Marc?* I was confounded. I never asked this woman if she knew 'Marc' because I thought I was simply picking up the name from the last reading. So I continued on thinking to myself that perhaps I should have meditated and smudged longer. I was getting frustrated and distracted with the peculiarity of it all.

I could see the letters clearly in my mind's eye and, I knew they spelled 'Marc.' I didn't however completely trust my own messages or judgment at that point in time and what I learned next was a lesson I've never since forgotten. It was a lesson in trusting my inner voice—and what I pick up in visions and messages. I revealed everything else to this woman except the name Marc and at the end of the reading the young eyes looked into mine and softly inquired, "Could I please ask you a question?"

"Of course you can," I answered. Right at that moment I could hear the name Marc again come through my mind loud and clear.

She leaned over and asked, "Do you see me marrying my boyfriend?" I paused for a moment and suddenly had a vision of the name Robert and told her so straight away. She screeched out loud and threw her hands up in the air.

"Robert! That was my last boyfriend. He still loves me

but I don't love *him* any more." She quickly reached into her purse to fetch out a picture of her boyfriend and, before I could say another word, handed me the photo. It was encased in a miniature silver frame. "*This* is my boyfriend," she asserted.

I pulled my specs back down over my eyes to have a better look, and before I even saw his face, I could see the name at the bottom of the little picture. Black faded ink, spelling the name 'Marc.' I smiled and said, "Greta, you may not believe this, but I saw this name in your reading and, spelled the exact same way!" It was a great lesson for me. I learned that no matter how ridiculous or weird these things seem, they are coming through for a reason! And, consequently, they have to be mentioned. I was thankful that I was picking up the right name for the right person after all, but was disappointed that I didn't trust my own inner voice. The lesson I learned from that reading was that no matter how uncanny it may sound, feel or seem, when messages are coming through—especially when I hear them clearly—there is no doubt as to their significance! I had to learn to mention them, no matter how absurd or unrelated they may seem at the time.

From that day on—and throughout the chapters of this book—unusual, extraordinary, heart warming, intriguing and unexplainable stories related to such incidences abound. These stories are where people's lives have changed, where miracles have taken place and, where destiny comes knocking. The universe, with all of its many and mysterious wonders, plays a big part in all of our lives. I realized I was no longer reluctant to say what I was picking up. I refer to it now as my 'Ultimate Lesson.'

Chapter 7

Proving Myself To Sceptics

There are still times when I have had to prove myself before my client ever sits down in my chair. For instance, and not long ago, I had a very skeptical client who began testing my abilities—and accuracy—from the minute I talked to her on the phone. The first words out of her mouth were, "You probably won't be able to read me, because no other reader has ever been able to. And, I've been to dozens." She snorted as she finished the statement. I've learned over the years not to allow any negativity to influence my energy. So ignored her statement, and made her an appointment for later that day.

She was half hour early, which surprised me for someone who was reluctant about having a reading, and when I asked, "Are you ready for a reading"? Her reply was; "Well, sort of, I guess. I don't like anything negative or alarming, but there is *something* I would like to know about." She was squeezing her hands together as if she was going to start praying for a miracle. I was easily able to sense her anxiety, so before leading her into my reading room, I left the decision up to her.

"Well Laurie, if you are ready, we can get started."

Almost immediately I could pick up her nervousness and skepticism. I wouldn't have been the least bit surprised if she had said something like, "I can't go through with it." Her aura was dull and dark. She was full of anger, negativity, fear, and seemingly low self esteem. I felt certain that once I got her seated in my cosy reading room the arranged atmosphere there would offer her some much needed tranquility. Calming sounds of trickling water from my corner fountain combined with the soft serenading sounds of recorded flute music. My majestic fig tree, which appears to enjoy a regal command of the room, compliments the water and audio ambiance. The overall effect was enough to put anyone in a relaxing mood or, at the very least, a better one than which they arrived with!

She showed no further signs of hesitation and as soon as we entered the room Laurie found herself one of my most comfortable chairs directly beside my stone and crystal collection. She seemed somewhat fascinated with it however she was more focused on scrutinizing the room itself. I lit a vanilla scented votive candle which sat upon my antique mahogany table. I had, moments earlier, placed a vase there with some fresh-picked Tiger-Lillies from my garden. I felt confident that the atmosphere I had created in my reading room was sufficient to bring even this reluctant client to a higher, and more relaxed, mental state. She was no longer sabotaging my energy level which gave me the opportunity to make some progress with her. The other benefit was that once I had subdued her anxieties somewhat, I was able to give her a much more accurate reading. Laurie was in her mid-forties and very attractive. She was tall, dark-haired, and had vivid marlin-blue eyes that projected a certain depth. The intensity of this color alone would normally captivate anyone, but it also emanated a distant emptiness. I noticed as well that they ra-

Chapter 7 • Proving Myself to Sceptics

diated a degree of cold apprehension. I realized I could have given her a reading by just looking into her eyes! Her aura was dark and weary and she gave me a subliminal yet distinct impression that she didn't want to be read. I calculated that she had come to see if I was going to be able to break through the unreadable label she had so doggedly claimed for herself. I was convinced she wanted me to tell her something she in fact already knew—to prove some kind of point or something. After a few minutes of chit-chat, I held out my hands to take hers, so we could get started with her reading.

She had a surprisingly grip and she wasted no time telling me what was on her mind. "I have a bad aura don't I? Every reader says that I do. What color of aura do you see around me?" Her firm grip had now transformed into a vice grip. "Is it black or grey?" she inquired in a demanding voice.

Before Laurie could ask any more negative questions, I interjected with something to the effect of, "If you could just sit quietly so as not to interrupt my energy, I better have the ability to sense any messages that may be trying to come through. I can only pick up your energy if you're calm. Try to be open to what I am going to tell you, whether it is good or whether it is not."

"I'm sorry. Really I am," she replied apologetically. "I will keep quiet. You can count on it!" I closed my eyes and we sat silently holding hands until I could pick up her energy and listen to spirit and my guides.

"I'm seeing a baby. A baby who is no longer with us—she has passed over to the other side. She died an instant death—a crib death." I could feel the energy of this baby right in the room with us. "She is trying to tell you something Laurie."

"I can't believe you see the child I lost to crib death. This is unbelievable. What about her? What else can you tell me?" she cried out.

"She wants you to know she is happy and not to blame yourself for not being there when she died."

Smiling, I said, "You are going to be able to communicate, because you will now hear messages from her. She will be of more help to you now as an angel than she would have been if she had lived."

"What do you mean by that?" Laurie inquired, as she sat, glimmering in an aura of hope.

"It means she is your spirit companion and will always be with you wherever you go—she will guide you. She is without any doubt *your* angel!" We both reached for a tissue and wiped away tears.

Not wanting to go any further with the reading at this point Laurie said, "I'm sorry that I was so negative at first. I hope you will forgive me."

"Don't apologize dear," I said. Many people are skeptical until something comes through in their reading—something that confirms the authenticity of the reader."

"My goodness, I'm feeling as though I've just had a visit with my daughter that I lost so long ago. I've got goose bumps." she exclaimed, still wiping away tears.

"That's because she is here with us right now in spirit. You can talk to her any time you want, because only her body is gone. Her spirit is with you always and everywhere"

Laurie hugged and thanked me. "I came to you today, because I needed to know that she is happy and that it wasn't my fault she died."

This girl was not hard to read, she just had to be open

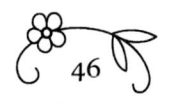

to anything that was going to come through. Once she realized she could trust me, and felt comfortable that I was not someone she needed to be guarded with, her apprehension quickly dissipated, vanished even. Laurie then opened herself up to a much higher level, and was able to then be read the way most people who believe in psychics are read. We exchanged another hug goodbye, and the last thing I remember her saying to me as she went out the door was, "Thank you for giving me faith again. Faith in psychics, faith in myself and, faith in God. And thank you more than any words can say for making me aware that my daughter is right beside me all the time, and that she is my guardian angel and my spirit guide."

Smiling I replied, "I'm only too glad to have helped you in any way."

Beaming with happiness, a warm glow radiated upon her face. With a sparkle in her eyes she made her way to the door.

"Well, I know one thing. You will sure be seeing me again! My image of psychics before, I have to admit, was that they were all in it for the money. After meeting you today and getting such an emotionally poignant reading—and seeing that you don't want any money for it—I would have to say that psychics really are gifted and inspirational people. I'm honoured to have met you" With those parting words, I felt emotions run through me. It's a familiar sensation and one that I feel when I experience such heart-felt confirmations. It's always further confirmation for me that I am doing the work I was intended to do on this earth.

On Many occasions during the course of a reading I have had clients unknowingly stare into my eyes with the look of mistrust, suspicion, skepticism or cynicism. Sometimes, it's a combination of all these. They don't realize of course that I can pick up on all of this negative energy they are feeling simply by looking back into their eyes. Their demeanor, posture, and movements, are very much a part of what I pick up in the energy that flows or doesn't flow around them. Their body-language is an intrinsic part of it all. I know that the first words out of my mouth have to be something they can relate to or they quickly put up their guard. From then on I have to prove myself to them. Luckily this usually happens only a matter of minutes into a client's reading and it is only because I have picked up something they can relate to—something that *only* they knew about.

A good example of this occurred when I had a very busy day at the salon where I was giving weekly readings—every Monday. One particular evening I just wanted to go home and put my feet up with a cold glass of ice-tea and ponder the day's events. I quickly realized that would have to wait when a good looking man in his early twenties walked in and asked very politely, "Hi. My name's David, do you happen to have time for a half hour reading?"

Glancing at my watch and seeing that it was almost closing time, I answered him with, "I have time for a half hour reading—but that is all."

He replied with a calm vagueness, "I don't really believe in this kind of thing, but..."

"But what?" I inquired. "You either want to get read, or you don't. It doesn't make any difference to me." Before he could answer, I added, "Why are you here?"

"Uh,...well, because," he smirked, "I just thought I would find out if you can see anything that might help me and, you have read my mom before. She wanted me to come here for a reading. She speaks highly of you."

Chapter 7 • *Proving Myself to Sceptics*

"But do *you* want to see me?" I inquired, curiously. "Because if you want, you can think about it and come back when you make your mind up."

"No, I don't think that will be necessary. I'd really like you to read me today if you could."

"Okay," I answered softly. "Come along then and let's get started."

He followed me into my small and make-shift reading room at the back of the salon. Queries were coming, one after the other, even before we sat down. His first question was, "How can I know what you're going to tell me is true?"

"Well David," I said, "I guess you will just have to trust me." We began the reading and nothing seemed to make sense to him or me in the initial moments.

The name Michele came up a couple times, which prompted David to confidently state, "I don't know *anyone* with that name. My girlfriend's name is Penny, so it just doesn't apply to me whatsoever."

Ignoring his comment, I contiunued. "You will settle down, get married, and have two girls."

"You see *me* settling down?" he replied, with an almost detached undertone. "I kind of doubt it right now but, it's a nice thought I guess."

I stayed the course with what I was picking up. "You will get a job driving heavy equipment. I see a big yellow *Caterpillar*. Could be a grater or a front-end loader, or something of the sort."

"But, I can't see that. I can't see that because I work in construction—I've never driven heavy equipment and nor do I intend to either."

I soldiered on with, "You are going to move away from BC and work in Alberta."

With a gasp and a half-laugh he spoke as if what he was saying was an indisputable fact, "I don't like the cold weather and it get's to 35 below there during those long winter months. That is one of the last places I would want to go! This I know for sure. And besides, my girlfriend would never let me go there *even to work,* so I m sorry, but nothing of what you are saying makes any sense at all."

"Perhaps it doesn't make sense to you right now David," I offered, "but before long you will likely be able to relate to most, if not all of these things. You have to put trust in yourself—and have faith in the universe—before things in your life will change for the better."

Seemingly satisfied with this thought, and determined to trust in himself after my lecture on his attitude of negativity, he left the shop with his notes in hand. As he was leaving he surprised me a little with a quick but genuine hug. "I will let you know if anything happens relative to your predictions." I smiled and bid David good-bye, thinking all the while that he'd be back.

It wasn't long after this reading that David sent his sister in for a reading. She appeared a cheerful soul and was more than delighted to pass some interesting information on about her brother. In fact, she was quite excited to tell me.

"We can't believe how your reading literally changed his life! He went from being bored with his life; from being a small town guy, to moving away to the big city of Calgary—a place that made no sense to him at the time of his reading. He has found a new girlfriend there and, incredibly, with the name Michele—just like you said. Can you believe they're planning on getting married in the Spring" David wanted me to tell you as well that he did get a job driving a big yellow loader—for an excavating company. Believe it or not, he is even getting used to the freezing temperatures!" She was laughing while telling me all this and I laughed along with her. We were both fascinated with his timing and the fact that all these events took place within the year. Before her reading she told me, "I know one thing for sure. You don't have to prove *anything* to me like you did my brother!"

Chapter 8

TRUSTING MY INNER VOICE

Learning to completely trust my inner voice and act upon it without hesitation or doubt was something that didn't happen overnight. It took many years and many life threatening situations before I acted upon them with automatic and instant reactions.

One of those times was one winter while vacationing in Palm Springs California. I was there doing readings, enjoying the sun, the swimming, and all the sights with my husband. I had a very strong feeling all week long of wanting to invite my parents down for a few weeks to enjoy some of the nice weather with us. I made up my mind to invite them. My husband was totally fine with this decision and arranged to pick them up from the airport as soon as they could get away from Vancouver.

During the first month everything was absolutely beautiful; the weather was in the 80s every day. We stayed in a gorgeous 2-bedroom apartment, with a view of the desert which was so vibrantly scattered with blooming cactus and wild flowers that it kept me snapping my camera from sun up to sun down.

From early morning we all planted ourselves somewhere around the swimming pool, with our coffee and

Chapter 8 • *Trusting My Inner Voice*

newspaper in hand, not wanting to do much except soak up all the sun. Coming from British Columbia in January, we had happily left a foot of snow behind us and we didn't want to waste a minute of perfect weather, shopping in malls, or spending time inside the suite.

The second month was equally great as far as the weather went, but I kept getting this awful feeling that something was not so right with my mom; On this one particular day I had a vision of her being in a hospital bed and having surgery. I was deeply worried that she had something seriously wrong with her. I didn't want to alarm her or get her worried about anything since she was having such a relaxing time enjoying her surroundings. She was also able to enjoy a nice visit with a granddaughter and great granddaughter who had driven in from the Orange County area, so I knew this was not the best time to ask her any questions about her health. She looked great, and said she felt fine, so why was I getting these messages that my mom was not fine? I tried to block it out, by swimming in the pool most of the day, reading for new clients, and writing in my journal but, alas, none of this worked. I was still plagued with these thoughts of mom being sick, and as the days passed I was getting more visual pictures of her being in the hospital, and had the word cancer pop into my head more than once.

I knew after not sleeping soundly or being able to concentrate on anything that it was ruining my vacation, and that it was something that needed to be quickly addressed. I felt I had no other choice except to just come right out and say what I was feeling—what my inner voice was telling me. I waited until we were sitting down poolside the next morning after my niece had left. Very calmly I said, "Mom, when was the last time you had a complete physical?"

She glanced up from the newspaper she was reading and said, "Oh, I just had one about a month ago, why do you ask?" she inquired with a worried look on her face.

I lifted my sunglasses to see her more clearly, and asked, "Did you get a clean bill of health?"

Looking back down at the newspaper she answered with, "I'm happy to say yes I did. In fact the doctor even examined my breasts and said I have no lumps or anything. Everything was good."

All I could think of to say at that point was, "Well, sometimes they can be wrong. Maybe you should get a second opinion."

"Now why would I want to get a second opinion if I already have a clean bill of health?" she said with a look of concerned puzzlement.

"Because I have a little voice inside me saying that the doctor might have missed something. And besides," I added convincingly, "What would it hurt anyway—we don't pay for the exam, and it would make me feel a lot better knowing that you really are healthy."

Looking more terrified than ever because she knew how my visions and little voices sometimes turn out, she said, "Very well then. When we get back home next month I will do that if it will make you happy."

"Thanks mom. It will make me feel better!"

That night when I went to bed I tossed and turned all night long. I never slept a wink, because I could see us all returning back to Canada before our vacation was up. I knew then the doctor did not diagnose my mom properly, and that she would be in the hospital bed I had seen her in. My stomach felt sick and when my husband asked, "Why are you tossing and turning—what's wrong?" I had to tell him what was on my mind.

Chapter 8 • Trusting My Inner Voice

"I'm worried about Mom," I whispered.

"Why?" he asked, half asleep and somewhat confused.

"Because I have a very bad feeling she has cancer." What he said next didn't really surprise me, but it was indeed the comforting words I needed to hear just then. Even though he was half asleep, his compassion and logic were clear.

"If your mom is seriously ill, like you are feeling she is, then don't worry about our vacation. We've been here almost two months anyway, and as much as it would be nice to stay for the three months like we planned, your mom's well-being is more important." I kissed him for his commendable compassion. His words really meant the world to me. "Have you mentioned anything to your mom yet?" he asked calmly.

"No, not yet, but I have to tell her tomorrow because I don't want to keep putting it off; she's agreed to have another check-up as soon as we get back home."

I remember laying there, asking my angels for a miracle of some kind so we could get through this tough time that I knew in my heart was likely on the horizon.

The next day was truly an answer to my prayers, when my Mom right out of the blue, while sipping her morning coffee poolside, announced, "I sure would like to go shopping for a new bathing suit today." I almost jumped out of my chair with excitement, knowing that this would give me the perfect opportunity for opening up the subject of a breast exam. I didn't give her any chance to change her mind either. I hurriedly prepared a light breakfast and before we knew it we were in the midst of tourists shopping on the famous Palm Canyon Drive. While we were sitting at an outdoor patio having a bite to eat and a cold drink, I nonchalantly got to the subject of my inner-voice. I knew she was curious but I also knew she didn't want to inquire.

I started with, "Mom I'm so glad that you're going to get a second opinion with another check-up."

She took a deep breath and said, "Well I sure hope everything is alright." We finished our lunch and began wandering through the seemingly endless array of fashion boutiques so that she could try on some bathing suits. I helped her select ones that were fashionable and suitable for her figure and age. Each time she tried one on she would call me over to have a look, to get my opinion just as most mothers and daughters do.

It wasn't until she came out of the dressing room wearing a suit that I had picked out for her that was far too revealing, I don't know why it popped into my hands, I should have known the style was not her at all. It was solid black, had a very revealing gathered bodice, and was eye-catching to say the least, but what it exposed to me was a very obvious lump that was under the skin about 3 inches below the collar bone. My heart pounded as I looked closer. While I was doing so—undoubtedly with a look of concerned look upon my face—Mom said, "What are you looking at?"

Maintaining as calm a composure as I could, I replied, "It's a lump Mom, and I don't like the look of it. Didn't you say your doctor did a breast exam, and that he said he felt no lumps?"

"Yes that's what I said; he did do a breast exam, and had said he didn't feel any lumps"

Shaking my head and feeling a surge of anxiety I realized the shopping would have to wait. "Let's leave the bathing suit for another day Mom. I think right now we have to get back to Canada."

"Back to Canada!" she exclaimed with a sullen annoyance. Is it that bad?" I knew her next question was going

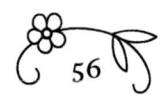

Chapter 8 • Trusting My Inner Voice

to be exactly what she said, "You don't think its cancer do you?"

All I could think of was to offer a truthful answer, "I can't lie to you mom, I know that it likely is."

She started to cry and hugged me with trembling arms. Her disposition was not unlike it would have been had she just received a life sentence. Her panic and apprehension were understandable to say the least. I did my best trying to keep my composure but it wasn't easy, since a big knot was at the same time tying itself to the pit of my stomach. Calming my Mom down was my biggest challenge.

"Mom, I see you living to be a very ripe old age, and healthy too!" I remarked with all the confidence I could muster. My immediate goal was to bring the color back to her face.

She smiled at me and proclaimed, "I'm glad you are the psychic in the family, because I need to believe you."

We ended up leaving the Palm Desert resort the following weekend, after explaining to the management that being an intuitive reader compels me to trust my instincts. They seemed genuinely curious about my line of work. I was further convinced when the wife of the couple who ran the resort inquired with particular interest, "Will you keep in touch? When you come back, we can refer you to many clients who I'm sure will want to be read by you."

We left the golden sun, warm temperatures, the great sights and people we were just getting to know. The accompanying downcast mood was eclipsed by a great desire to get back home in order to expedite treatment for my Mom. Not surprisingly, we had a quiet and somewhat stressful trip back home to Vancouver. For me it was worsened by the fact that I realized Mom would be undergoing surgery as well as the treatments that typically go along with breast cancer.

By the following week, Mom had completed a battery of blood tests as well as another mammogram which confirmed everyone's suspicions. The course of treatment was a lumpectomy rather than a mastectomy—which we were all so thankful for—followed by twenty-three weekly radiation treatments, including the anti-cancer drug *Tamoxifin.*

The following winter we decided to go back to the very hotel suite where we stayed the year before, at the *North Palm Canyon Inn.* We felt it would be only fitting to ask mom and dad to join us once again. Needless to say by then we were all ready for a real relaxing holiday. We stayed for an enjoyable—and therapeutic—three months. When I wasn't writing, I was reading clients from all over the world. Some of which you will read about in this book!

On another occasion several years later, I had to trust my inner voice once again. I was in Vancouver visiting my friends and family. For the life of me, I couldn't figure out why I was feeling kind of anxious, even though I had just enjoyed a fun-filled day with good food, great old friends and my loving family. Even with such a perfect day unfolding around me I was overcome by an uneasy feeling. A feeling that something was wrong washed over me just as it had with my Mom not long before. This time it was a feeling about my oldest niece who lived in California. I knew I had to see her and give her a reading. From there, I knew I could determine more. I had no similar feelings of this when she had spent the day with us in Palm Springs the month before. I didn't know whether to simply call her to tell her what I was feeling, or to fly down to California and tell her in person. I had thoughts of possibly worrying her for something insignificant as well. What if she were to come all the way up to Canada to see me and it wasn't anything serious! I couldn't do that to her. I tried to tell myself it was likely nothing important, and that I could very well be jumping to conclusions. But the thought that something was terribly wrong, continued to overcome me. I soon realized I was at the point where I couldn't enjoy the rest of my time in Vancouver. I knew I had to call my niece.

Once again, I summoned the confidence I needed to trust my inner voice. I picked up the phone and, somewhat dazed, I dialed her number. With so many troubling thoughts racing through my mind at the time, it took a number of unanswered rings before I realized she was not home. *Now what?* I began thinking to myself. Frustrated that I couldn't immediately get a hold of her, I decided to call her mother. After some idle chatter I said, "We sure had a nice visit with Michele in Palm Springs last month" I was wondering if she would allow me to read her over the phone, or maybe next time she is in town"

"Really—why is it that you want to read her? You have never read family before—Is something wrong?"

"No, there is nothing wrong. I just feel I need to talk to her." I replied, realizing she sensed something was up—something that I wasn't saying.

"I will pass it along to her, but you might be able to talk to her in person yourself next week since she has decided to come up for one of her friend's birthdays."

"Oh great," I said, "I'll extend my vacation so that I can see her."

"You really do want to talk to her by the sounds of it," she interjected with more than a hint of curiosity in her voice.

"I'll look forward to catching up with you all soon. In the meantime, please have Michele call me as soon as possible at Julie's where I'll be staying."

"For sure I will, I'm sure she will be happy to talk to you.

Until then enjoy your vacation, and we will hopefully see you soon."

I felt better knowing that I had at least gone that far with this feeling, and knew that there was no turning back.

The next day my niece phoned, curious and interested that I had requested to talk to her. Her words were concise and right to the point, "Okay Aunty, what is up? You never ever read family and I'm family, so why do you want to read me? Do you see something bad? Am I going to be okay?" Typical questions under the circumstances, and I knew that I couldn't beat around the bush.

"Michele," I started, "you will be the first family member to have a reading by me."

She cut in with, "Thanks Aunty. I've always wanted to be read by you and, I feel honored to be the first family member you chose. On the other hand, I hope it's going to be a positive reading with nothing that is going to trouble me."

"Michele, don't get yourself worried for no good reason—it may be urgent, but just the fact that I'm going to read you now, is a good thing in itself."

"Okay, I'm convinced," she said. "I will come to see you as soon as I arrive. I'll come over to Aunty Julie's where you can give me my reading. I can't wait!" We said goodbye with the usual affection, and I took a deep breath knowing that I just took another giant step towards trusting my inner voice.

The rest of the week went by very quickly; I cancelled my appointments back home in Vernon, and made a flight reservation to fly home the following week.

When Michele called to say she was in town, and that she was on her way over for her reading, my sister Julie

Chapter 8 • Trusting My Inner Voice

and I quickly realized the freshly painted in-law-suite situated in the lower-level of her home would be perfect for this very special reading. I hadn't ever read there before, but being a new setting was of no disadvantage. My sister and I arranged the room with a serene ambiance of lit candles, fresh cut flowers, soft music and nice comfy tub-styled chairs for us to sit in. We had just finished the setting when we heard the door bell, and no psychic powers were needed to know who it was!

You could hear the happy exchanges and elation of our greetings a block away I'm sure. We are a true-blue typical Italian family when it comes to greetings. As we led Michele down the hallway to the stair well that led to the basement, she was open-minded and inquisitive, "This is kind of scary, but I'm really ready for whatever it is you are going to tell me, so don't hold anything back because I want to know everything—and I mean everything!"

"I will only be able to relay to you the messages I receive and the visions I may get. You can interpret whatever you want from it," I answered back.

My sister left us alone so we could have total privacy, and as we sat close together readying ourselves for the reading, I spoke almost instantly, "Michele, right now I'm picking up the female organs, the uterus and ovaries. I feel that they need to be checked, and that if you don't see a doctor right away, this could most definitely turn to something much more serious." Looking at me with her big brown eyes, she asked, "Are you sure?"

"Yes, I am sure."

"Do you mean that I should go to a doctor up here in Canada, or wait until I get back to California?"

While not wanting to alarm her anymore than I already had, I nonetheless delivered her the messages as soon as

I was picking them up, "Michele, I think you should go to the family doctor you had before you moved to the States. Make an appointment with him while you are here in Vancouver, so that you can go back home knowing what the problem is."

"Aunty, you really seem sure that something is wrong because you don't say, *if* there is a problem, you say what the problem *is*. I know you won't tell me if it is something really bad, so I won't even ask, but I can tell by the look on your face Aunty that you are worried, and that is enough for me to phone today for a doctor's appointment."

"I see you with a little girl someday though," I said cheerfully, "so it's not all bad news."

"Taking a very deep breath and exhaling, a big sigh of relief, she remarked, "That is very good news...because I would like to have at least one child in my life."

"You will, but right now focus on what you need to."

"You're right Aunty; I *will* go to see my old doctor, because now I have to know what is wrong before going back home."

"Good plan Michele," I said as I jumped to my feet. "Now let's go upstairs and have a cup of tea, so you can have a visit with Aunty Julie."

I had the strongest feeling that this was one time I had to trust my intuition, inner voice, gut feelings, premonition, or anything you wanted to call it. I had to believe in the voices I heard, and the visions I was having. I didn't want to lose someone just because I didn't have trust in my inner voice, because I knew I would never be able to live with myself if something happened to any of my loved ones, just because I was afraid to speak up and say what I hear, feel, or see.

Chapter 8 • Trusting My Inner Voice

The next day I was waiting by the phone to hear how soon Michele could get in to see the doctor, and sure enough she got an appointment for the next day. I knew in my heart that she wasn't going to die, but I also knew that the words pre cancer were going to come up in the tests she would have. It was just another case where I had to trust my inner voice because it was so strong.

Just before my departure to fly home, all Michele's test results came in, and the doctor had her go to his office to have them explained to her. When Michele called to tell me the results, she announced, "Aunty, you were right. The Dr said, "If you are planning on having a baby, you better have one as soon as possible, because you have pre-cancerous tissue of the cervix."

"I'm not surprised Michele," I said with sympathy, "What else did he tell you?"

"He told me I have a few different options to consider and he gave me a list of them to consider and inquire about when I get home."

"I'm so happy for you Michele that you have a choice of treatments, and that you are going to be fine."

"Aunty, I was so happy to hear of these options, because it means I can still have a baby and, you did say you saw me with a baby, so I know I will have one!"

As Michele was contemplating her treatment options, she met the man of her dreams, married him several months later, and had a beautiful baby girl. Which Dr's were sure it was a boy. I had a vey clear vision of her not with a boy, but a cute little girl, so sure in fact that two months before she gave birth I mailed her a little leopard dress and matching hair ribbon. At the time everyone said, but she is having a boy', I continued to say, "I only see a girl"

Janeah Rose • Reflections of a Psychic

Trusting my inner voice became a big part of my life, especially when it proved to save my own life in the '80s. I was married for ten years and still with very high hopes of getting pregnant. I had a beauty salon set up in my home at the time with my reading room in another part of the house. I also had a hobby and craft room where I spent many hours creating, building, sewing, and painting. It was in this craft room that I could detach myself from the world at large and forget about everything except what I was working on. One particular day I was working away canning peaches from one of our many fruit trees when I had this vision of myself in a hospital bed. I didn't appear sick in any way—I actually looked better than I ever did. In fact, the same month I was experiencing these visions, I had a photo taken of me at the photographers, and to this day is one of the best pictures I've ever had taken. I found myself doing things around the house that were in preparation for when I would be in the hospital as well as for when I returned home from the hospital. I was actually doing all this subconsciously without realizing it, I found myself organizing my dresser drawers so that my husband could readily find exactly what I wanted him to bring for me. It seemed crazy at the time, and I thought for sure my husband Steve was going to think I was nuts if I told him what I was doing. But, after a few weeks, I finally had to tell him what it was I was feeling, and, more importantly, *why* I was acting so strange.

I was relieved to hear him say, "Well you should know your intuition by now—you seem to know them for everyone else."

I was happily flattered by his straight-out display of confidence in me. "Thank-you for not thinking I'm completely crazy."

Chapter 8 • *Trusting My Inner Voice*

"If you're picking up any indications what so ever that something is wrong with you, then there more than likely is."

"Your right Steve, but I will have to make up some kind of story for my doctor; otherwise I won't have a legitimate reason to go in for a check up."

Later that same day I made the phone call, somewhat nervous as to what I would say if they inquired what it was regarding. Luckily, they didn't ask too many questions, and by the next day, I was in my doctor's office with a well thought out story. When the doctor walked in and asked the standard question, "What may I help you with?" my heart started to pound since I had never before been a liar. I didn't know if I could actually pull it off, but I somehow managed to. I sat there just as if I was in a movie, acting out a rehearsed part. I knew that this would be the only way to get her attention. It somehow seemed as though someone else was doing the talking for me because the words flowed effortlessly. I felt as though I was a doctor too—talking to her about another patient. It was a bizarre experience. I was not surprised when she finally said, "I think you are due for a scraping of the uterus. I'm going to book you for this Friday."

A few days later I had the minor surgery for the scraping procedure. At that time they also did a Pap test. It was this test that I knew would confirm or neutralize my biggest worry. I could feel the sensation of barely perceptible tremors creeping through my comfort zone—almost as if I was standing on a geological fault-line. Simultaneously, a heavy weight felt as though it was precariously perched upon my shoulders. I laid there on the cot trying to distance myself from the associated worries, waiting for the doctor to say I could go home and await the results.

Of course, waiting for test results is the hardest part of the whole ordeal and, with respect to this, I was no exception. I knew that my results were going to be serious—and I was prepared for that. But I also knew that it wasn't going to be fatal. When I got home, I kept hearing my inner voice telling me to 'pack a few things for the hospital again, only this time for major surgery.' I continued to prepare by putting things in order for the days I'd be gone. I pre-made several dinners for hubby, got all my things together in a little night case, and made a few phone calls to family to apprise them of when I would be going in for surgery. When they asked, "What for?" I merely said, "A simple hysterectomy." No one needed to know the details.

On the Monday morning I got the phone call from the doctor's office telling me the results of the tests done in the hospital. I felt my heart sink since I knew that it meant I would no longer be able to dream of someday having a child of my own. It was a dream I often had, even though I knew deep in my heart of hearts that I wouldn't be a biological mother to any children.

The doctor's office visit was short and bittersweet. I had two options; having a complete hysterectomy, or having a piece of the cervix taken out which had the cancer. To me there was really no option. My inner voice kicked in once again, and instructed; "You need to get rid of the whole uterus, if you want to be forever free of the cancer."

So my answer to the doctor was very clear and to the point, "I'm electing to go with the hysterectomy." He didn't look surprised. In fact, he seemed to approve of my decision.

"You can go home and think about it if you want to." he offered.

Without any hesitation I reaffirmed my decision. "I don't need to think about it doctor, I've already made up my mind."

Chapter 8 • *Trusting My Inner Voice*

Admitting called me a few days later, and I was booked for that weekend before the doctor was scheduled for vacation. The following day after the surgery, another doctor was making the rounds for my doctor and when I asked "Why?" he said, "Your doctor was booked to go on vacation yesterday, but wanted to do your surgery before he left, because he thought it could spread from a #4 to a #5 which would be 'invasive cancer' by the time 2 weeks went by."

Shaking my head in disbelief, I said, "He sure is a special doctor." As I lay there that night I said my usual prayers, thanking God for watching over me, and a special prayer for Doctor Jordon, who I feel played a crucial part in saving my life, both on *and* off the operating table. It was just another time when I was glad I not only listened to my inner voice but also acted upon it. My angels are never wrong, neither are my premonitions.

Chapter 9

QUALITY TIME WITH FATHER

Sometimes the visions I get aren't always understandable at the time of the reading. Conversely, it's often I will announce that my vision is very clear along with all the smallest of details that come through right along with the event. However when it comes to determining the exact time an event will take place, I get confused because it doesn't have a time attached to it. I pick up the event itself, but not the timelines. Sometimes it will happen in a matter of hours, sometimes in a matter of days. Sometimes, its months. And, on some occasions, even a few years or more.

A good example of this was when I was in Arizona for the winter, in the early eighties. I was a typical snowbird from Canada enjoying the beautiful desert winters swimming, bike-riding, hiking, sitting under the palm trees, and, giving readings by the poolside. I was introduced to a lovely couple from Florida one morning while having a continental breakfast in the Resort where we were staying. Sometimes it pays to be an ease dropper, which is how I got to meet this couple, who had just been read by a psychic reader the day before and were talking about how she predicted many things from their past but nothing for their

Chapter 9 • Quality Time with Father

future. I felt it was meant to be that I was standing beside them in the lineup for our morning coffee and warm Danishes. So very non chalontly cut in with "That's unfortunate, I can see all kinds of good things around you both" almost dropping his plate of goodies, he said, "Are you a psychic reader"? Oh my Gosh" this is unbelievable" They were obviously ecstatic to be in the company of a psychic reader.. The two of them were business people who owned and operated a franchise of flower shops.

Olga was out-going, friendly and a bit lavish in some idiosyncratic ways, but still remarkably down to earth and fun to be around. Heinz, who looked to be much older, was noticeably more reserved but he had a sophisticated and distinguished sense about him. His demeanor was very much that of a ladies man. They both wanted to be read together, which is something I very rarely did,. However I thought that I would give it a try if for no other reason than the fact that they were so intent on it. We decided to sit in the courtyard just outside the Grand entrance to the Resort, which happened to be secluded due to the towering palms that encircled it. The other choice was poolside, but it offered less privacy. The early evening was starting to cool down to the low 70s, a much more comfortable temperature than the high 80s we had throughout most of the day.

Somewhat surprised, I found myself rather liking the idea of reading the couple together. Mostly I think because they had so many things they wanted answered. One of the practical benefits was that what one forgot to tell me, the other one would remember which of course can be quite amusing. I proceeded to start with holding their hands and closing my eyes. Before long I announced, "You have to make a trip to Germany because your dad is not well."

"Whose dad?" they both asked at the same time.

"Both of us have a father in Germany."

I opened my eyes and looked at Heinz and said, "Your dad, Heinz."

"We are going over there in June. We have already bought our tickets, I haven't been back in five years."

"Don't wait until June," I said, "You must go soon."

"How soon?" they asked in unison.

"I don't know how soon exactly, all I know is that you shouldn't wait until June."

"Are you sure you see him sick?" Olga inquired worriedly.

"Yes, I see him waiting for you both, and he is indeed sick."

"We had a whole lot more questions for you, but now none of them are important—at least not at the moment. I wish you knew exactly when we should leave though."

I gave Olga the most accurate response I could, "My timing is sometimes not right but, the event itself is. I'm sorry I can't be more specific with the timeline, I can only tell you not to wait until June. You must go in early spring, I see tulips and daffodils and wild flowers"

"I believe you are seeing something very serious," Heinz announced in his deep baritone voice. "We will have to make some adjustments to our vacation plans, and change our plane tickets—don't you think so dear?" he asked Olga, looking at her with one eyebrow raised.

"I guess so, but I wish we knew *when!*" she replied, obviously exasperated.

"We will go when the daffodils start blooming in Germany," Heinz announced, laughing and trying to put hu-

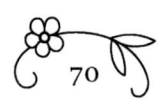

Chapter 9 • Quality Time with Father

mor in the reading. "This narrows it down at least. We will change our tickets for March, and stay for two months."

We ended the reading discussing some of their previous experiences with other psychic readers and, their accuracy. They kept telling me how they believe in Intuition and Destiny, and that nothing is a coincidence or a fluke"

"I'm sure there is a reason why we met you" Heinz asserted.

I said, "I'm sure there is a reason for everyone we meet and everything we do. I'm sure you won't be sorry that you've decided to go to Germany in the Spring instead of in June"

As they got up from their chairs, you could see the sadness in their eyes, and yet they still had a sense of humor saying; "Are you sure you don't want to come with us?"

"I wish" was my somber reply as I imagined being in Germany for a fleeting moment.

While Heinz got his pen and paper out from his pocket, Olga gave me a warm and gentle hug, saying, "We must get your address back in Canada so we can let you know how are trip went" I knew that I not only would be hearing from them again, but that I would also connect in person with them somewhere... someday...somehow...

I never heard from them again until about a year later, when I received a lovely card in my mail box postmarked Florida. I smiled and said under my breath "Olga and Heinz" They had written that they had went to Germany in March, visited with both of their families, had a wonderful time, and just before leaving decided to go to another city by train to visit friends. By the time they arrived at their friend's home in Munich, they got a call from Heinz's mother telling them that Heinz's father had just died. They returned back to the family home the very same day distraught and full of anger that they weren't with him when he died. However, after the immediate shock of the news set in, they both had time to reflect and be thankful—thankful that they had had the quality time with Heinz's dad before the end. They went on to mention that they felt he had not only waited for them to come home, but also for them to leave, before allowing himself to peacefully pass away. It was another one of those times when my timing was off—and I felt bad about it. I wished I could have been more accurate so that Heinz could have been sitting at his bedside when he passed.

Chapter 10

ONCE IN A LIFETIME

I've often thought that every psychic who has the visionary gift must have experienced this next story more than once. When I read people, the vision I typically have is not unlike the process of watching television. It is right in front of me, in vivid color. Often, the colors are bright and, this connection can sometimes last as long as the person is sitting in front of me. I love it because it never lets me down. You see what you see, and what you don't see doesn't usually happen. One of the clearest visions I have ever had to date captivated me as well as my client.

Her name was Karen. It was in the midst of the summer of '82—a remarkably hot one as I remember. I was meditating for a migraine headache when I heard someone at my door. I wasn't expecting anyone and my appointment book was clear for a change. I wondered if I was so lost in concentration that I just imagined the door-bell ringing. But as it rang again, for the second time, I realized there was someone there and I made my way down our formidable flight of twenty-four stairs and opened the door to this young blond girl whom I had never seen before. Upon sight of her I immediately realized she indeed had an appointment with me, only I had her scheduled for the wrong day. I quickly, and apologetically, explained this to her and she was very forgiving.

"Oh no problem —*do* you have the time to give me a reading today?"

"Of course I do Karen," I replied, "I have a very free day today, so actually, this will be great."

She was about twenty years of age and commanded a stunning presence. A slender bronze figure, weighing no more than 105 pounds soaking-wet, her honey-gold hair was cut in a feathered shag to the shoulders. Her face and eyes had a complex captivation to them. It was then, while studying her fabulous features, that I began to get a vision like I'd never experienced before.

She turned, smiled, and then proceeded to sit in my generously padded high-backed orange chair. My palm tree was situated directly beside her and the afternoon sun was casting a soft shadow from the palm. In the shaded light her face appeared even more complex than before, but her radiance was the same it seemed—in the light, or the dark. It was then that I had a vision of remarkable clarity. I couldn't help but feel with every bone in my body that this beautiful young girl sitting in front of me was going to be a top fashion model. She would travel the world! I continued to study her 'estilo,' style, that is. It was another extremly hot summer day—in the mid-thirties. Her attire reflected the temperatures. She was wearing loose-fitting mocha-collared satin shorts complimented by a matching fawn-brown silk tank-top. There was an attractive black satin sash casually tied about her waist. The ensemble, especially the sash, accented her small but athletic frame. Her waist looked no more than 23 inches. *She definitely has panache, this girl*, I thought to myself. As I prepared for her reading, she mentioned how she had heard of me.

Chapter 10 • *Once in a Lifetime*

"One of my friends told me about your background and said I should get read by you, but I'm a bit nervous... I've never done anything like this before."

"You're not alone feeling nervous for your first reading," I replied. "In fact, it's quite common. But don't worry, I know you are going to love what I'm about to tell you"

"Really? You can already feel that?" she enthused.

"No," I said, "I can already *see* that."

"Wow!" Karen squealed, with excitement. "And to think I almost changed my mind about coming to see you today."

"Well I know one thing Karen, this is one time you will be glad you didn't listen to your instincts."

"And why do you say that?"

"Why do I say that?" I repeated after her, "Because I think that your reading today is going to change your life big-time."

"I'm so looking forward to this!" she said, her eyes sparkling.

"Yes, now let's get started because I'm feeling as excited about this as you are!" I said as I handed her a paper and pen to take notes.

I started my reading with a bit faster pace than usual only because I didn't want to lose anything of the vision I was already seeing so clearly. Suddenly her auras glimmered like a concentric rainbow just above her head. At that moment a vision came cascading to me. I can still recall the intensity to this day and often it's as if I'm watching it all over again.

"I'm seeing images of you inside the pages of a glossy fashion magazine. I can see you upon a low-slung stage of some kind—two cameras with big lenses and power-winders are being given a workout. The energy on the set is intense; there is a flurry of pictures. It's definitely a professional photo-shoot and *you're* the focal point!"

As Karen sat there, captivated and listening intently, she was scribbling down the details of the scenario I was describing as fast as she could.

"You mean like modeling? You see me actually modeling? Professionally?"

"Yes! I see you in numerous styles of sleek swimwear—classic bikinis and sophisticated one-piece creations. This either means you will be traveling to somewhere in the tropics for a contracted photo-shoot or, you will be travelling the world spending a lot of time wearing swimwear!"

Fascinated beyond words, Karen's excitement grew in crescendo. She was having a hard time trying to stay calm.

"I can't believe that you see all this, but, you really do see this, don't you?"

"I sure do," I replied self-assuredly.

"Do you ever see things that don't happen?" Karen inquired.

Taking a deep breath, and breaking away from my vision I said, "Let's put it this way; when I see a vision as *clear* as this, they always come to pass."

"Wow. I'm so excited, but I just don't know if it could all happen to me." She shrugged. "Like, where would I get the money to travel? And, where would I go to get started? How can I ensure what you see will actually happen...I don't even know of any modeling agencies."

All these questions were coming out faster than I could catch my breath. The excitement endured simply because I didn't loose sight of the vision. I just kept getting more and more as she sat there looking at me, staring hopefully into my eyes. I continued seeing the same vision, and some of the peripheral details started to appear more clearly. "Karen, I'm seeing you in different poses and, in different photo-shoots. I see a camera upon a tripod with one of those big lenses the pros use. An oversized black umbrella is perched on top of it! Quite a few people are milling about behind the photographer. These shoots either have a lot of assistants, a curious gallery, or some of these people could simply be your on-location fan-club!"

I continued the reading for a half hour more, picking up parallel visions of Karen in her new career as a professional swimwear model. After she asked a few more questions like, "What do I do about the job I have now?" and, "Where will I move to?" I shrugged my shoulders and told her that even though it may be difficult for her to fathom at the moment, she would soon be seeing my vision as reality and, very likely, exactly the way I saw it. I mentioned that the timing I forecast isn't always as accurate as the vision.

"I would say your career change is going to be happening very soon indeed—in fact, it could be imminent. I have an excellent idea Karen. Tonight when you go to bed, try to visualize yourself as being a top model, posing in front of the camera. Imagine traveling all over the world. Picture yourself triumphantly walking on the white sandy beaches of famous and exotic tropical destinations; envision the sun on your face, and the cool turquoise water upon your feet. Then, if you have any doubts about anything, call me."

Karen was basking in the imagery I was relaying to her.

"Ask yourself if you are truly happy doing what you are doing right now and how long you plan on staying in the lifestyle you have now. Just working at a job you don't particularly love, that isn't really going anywhere—just making enough money to get by, paying the rent and bills. Ask yourself "Do I want to continue this line of work all my life." And "Do I love what I'm doing"?

"You're right—I don't really like my job. Actually, it's kind of boring." she said admittedly.

"Ask yourself if you would like to make a positive change in your life now while you are young and beautiful!" As fast as I was making these suggestions Karen was jotting them down in short hand, or a scribble she could re-write later. "When you have answered all these questions and have checked off nine out of ten, then have someone shoot an artistic little portfolio of you, with pictures wearing swimwear—one-piece bathing suits as well as bikinis. Then bring it to me because I want to see them *before* you become a star!"

Twisting her hair behind her ears, and folding her legs up underneath her to get more comfortable, I could see she was going to be staying for awhile. As she was writing, and trying to take all this information in, she kept saying, "You are unbelievable. In fact this whole reading seems so bizarre to me. It has always been like a dream of mine to model, only now that you have picked that up, actually seeing me becoming a model, well...now I want to just go for it, because it seems so much more realistic to me. And, you're right; I will go home and sleep on all of this. I need to try to digest what you've said and seen—I will get back to you and let you know how things are going, that I can promise you"

"You bet," I said with a smile. Our two-hour session was slowly coming to a close. "I will be waiting to not only hear from you, but I can't wait to see the results of the photo-shoot that you must arrange as soon as possible—I would like to go through them for you one by one, to show you

Chapter 10 • *Once in a Lifetime*

the particular image I see so clearly in my vision," I added as I got up from my chair.

"Oh you have just made my day" Karen exclaimed, giving me an exuberant hug in the process, "How can I ever begin to thank you? I'm so excited that I doubt I'll be able to sleep at all tonight! I'm going out right away to buy something really eye-catching for my pictures—I can't believe this is really happening." Before I could answer, she added, "A friend told me you were unreal, and now I know what she meant."

After gathering up her belongings, and putting some fresh lipstick on, she reached her arms out and gave me another hug saying, "You know what? I can just feel that something kind of magical happened here today, and that my life is never going to be the same. I can feel it tingling through my entire body. I never knew that going to a psychic could make a person feel so good. I have one more question before I go"? She said as she threw her purse over her shoulder... "Who do you see taking these pictures of me" "I see a friend who is just a good friend, who happens to be a male— I said jokingly, so have him take some really gorgeous pictures of you very soon, with some classic poses with great back-drops—just like in a studio. Take dozens if you have to, so you're more likely to capture that perfect shot."

"What do I do with these pictures—once I have them done I mean"?

"Well, first of all my dear girl, you're going to need them for advertizing—for promoting yourself that is. Portfolios are going to be an essential part of your new career."

"Portfolios." she repeated, "You mean those portfolios like the top models have?"

"Yes, that's exactly what I mean. If you are going to be a model, you will definitely need to create a professional looking one too! I may be able to help you with that. Karen, focus on what I have seen while you've been here; fashion swimwear, beaches, palm trees, and cameras in the tropics; I'm convinced it's something to do with the swimwear industry specifically."

"This is just so amazing, yet somehow I believe it to be true."

"Well believe it lucky girl, believe it. When I see it, I say it, and if I don't see it, I don't say it. So, yes you are going to be a top fashion model, because I not only see you in a magazine, but I also see myself reading it!"

Taking a deep breath, Karen remarked, "Well I can tell you one thing; if any of this happens, I will give you the first copy of the magazine. No, seriously—I truly will." And, at that moment, I truly believed her.

Feeling somewhat relieved that I finally had Karen not only convinced but full of enthusiasm as well, I said to her, "I hope you are ready for a whole new dynamic world waiting to unfold in front of you. This new chapter in your life will keep you very busy! But don't worry about that for you will love the lifestyle, the people, the challenges, the competitions, the cameras and photo shoots, and of course, the traveling. Some exotic locales are in store for you my dear girl"

Although still in a dazed state of disbelief, Karen nonetheless started projecting upon what lay ahead. "I would love to travel and see other parts of the world so that would be awhsome."

"I see you traveling more than you've ever dreamt," I replied. "To many tropical and breath-taking places. Plac-

Chapter 10 • Once in a Lifetime

es where the water shimmers in shades of turquoise, and where the sandy beaches are untouched, white, pristine, and secluded. And you are there."

"Wow," she remarked serenely. "You sure must trust your visions."

"Well Karen, I said, I have to tell you that I am trusting my visions today more than I ever have in the past, simply because I see everything so clearly. I wouldn't be telling you to go and take a bunch of pictures of yourself, if I didn't feel so certain that you had to."

"Really? I think I better go now and buy myself a really good camera, and have my friend take some of these pictures!"

"Excellent idea," I said, as I accompanied her down the walkway, "Make sure you bring me the pictures before you send them anywhere—so I can see the one you should focus on—the one that is your ticket"

Looking me straight in the eye, and scratching her head with a look of sheer confusion, she asked, "But where is it exactly I'm supposed to send these photos"? "You will find the answer to that within three weeks".

As she walked slowly out to her car, as if not really wanting to leave she turned and said, "I'm so thankful I met you, thank you so much for the reading, you'll definitely be seeing me very soon, like probably next week." She laughed.

As I watched her pull out of the driveway, I couldn't help but visualize that one day she would be driving the best car or cars that money could buy, and that I would someday sit beside her in one of those cars.

I had the distinct feeling that this was going to be something that might only happen once in a lifetime, so, I decided to record and document all coming and related events that would no doubt be surrounding this beautiful girl from this day forward.

Shaking my head and taking a deep breath, I realized that this vision would have to wait until the next reading, since Karen was by now halfway down the street. I could sense the energy she was feeling on her ride home. She was on cloud nine and so she should be. Anybody with that kind of destiny should be literally floating above the clouds.

About a week later I was busy with my yearly chore of making raspberry juice. The counter top was covered with canning jars, berries, pots and pans, and just plain mess. Juice from freshly pressed berries was ready to boil when the phone rang. Not wanting to answer it with sticky hands, I hesitated until the third ring. It was then I knew it was going to be Karen. I quickly rinsed off my red hands and grabbed the phone off the receiver. I knew the voice like I knew the face—both were indeed unforgettable.

"Hi Mary, its Karen, I have the pictures. They look pretty good. When is a convenient time to come see you? I can't wait to know what you think!"

"Fantastic Karen," I answered, "Come on over whenever you want. I'm anxious to see them."

"I can come by now if that's okay"

"It's fine with me, I said in a dither, forgetting all about the raspberries that were waiting to go into the processor. I tried to carry on with the juicing, but didn't get very far when I heard a voice calling my name over the outside intercom saying, "Hi, I'm here!"

"Come on in," I hollered, and at that she came running up the stairs. When I met her at the top landing she greeted me with a big friendly hug, as if we were long lost friends.

Chapter 10 • Once in a Lifetime

As she flipped open the oversized envelope of her freshly printed photographs, she remarked, "I'm actually quite amazed because they turned out better than I had anticipated."

She handed them all over to me. I reached for my reading glasses and said, "Let me pour us a couple of cold ice-teas. We'll sit out on the deck where we can go through these one by one while enjoying a cold drink" With ice-teas in hand, we made our way out onto the deck where the sun was finally going down, and where there seemed to be a nice summer breeze.

The first thing Karen said was, "You know if someone would have told me that I would be sitting with a psychic woman, sifting through some modelling photos of me, I would have told them they were nuts, absolutely nuts." As my contented new found friend sat comfortably sipping her ice-tea, I began perusing the glossy images. It was only moments later when I had a very clear vision—and it was one Karen very much liked the sound of.

"I see you wearing designer everything from head to foot." I said matter-of-factly. You will have an array of beautiful shoes and endless name brand accessories to match!" I had to stop myself from seeing further into that vision, as she wasn't here for a reading, she was merely here to show me the results of her first photo-session with her friend.

"What do you think of this one, or this one?" was the basis of the conversation for the most part. I was practically speechless as I went through them, because I knew for sure these very pictures were going to change Karen's life forever.

As I continued looking through them, one in particular popped out like none of the others. It was almost identical to the image in my vision. I will never forget it. The vision of that picture is one I still see in my mind's eye even to this day! I held it for a moment, visualizing its details. I just knew it would be the face that the fashion houses and their respective scouting agents would go nuts for. The picture itself was stunning. She wore a striking leopard print tank top. It was a head shot and she was looking straight into the camera. Her hair was wind-blown. It had a sexy look to it, there was no doubt of that. And yet, the overall effect was more than that. There was an elemental mystique about her 'look.' She possessed the kind of eyes cameras never get tired of. As an added bonus, she had little make-up and the result imparted a natural aura to the captivating beauty. It was in fact the same image I had seen in my vision the first time I ever met Karen. I instinctively knew it had to be *the* picture she needed for her portfolio cover—the one that she needed at this particular time at least.

As I held the glossy print in my hands, still contemplating the energy and aura she radiated, I happily announced, "I know this picture is going to change your life."

With the softest and most modest voice I've ever heard, she replied, "You know something...I can actually *feel* like my life is going to change now too. I feel it in every cell of my body. I have been getting shivers thinking about it."

We finished sipping our ice teas and perusing the photos. I set aside the most important of the bunch and we wrapped up our visit. Karen left shortly after saying, "I'm going to send copies of this picture in to modeling agencies—because you never know, right?"And you're never wrong right? She laughed.

The modeling, the magazines, the traveling, the competitions, money and bright lights, and everything else I have since seen of Karen from the first day I met her was not un-

Chapter 10 • *Once in a Lifetime*

like watching a movie. Only this time, it was even better, because the star of the movie was standing right in front of me! I was so excited for this beautiful young girl who was barley out of high school, and with so much potential—including intelligence. With so many doors wide open for her it was mind boggling even to me.

The next day, I was getting ready for a trip to Vancouver when the phone rang. I had this very distinct feeling that it was Karen calling to tell me some more exciting news. I picked up the phone and could barely say hello before an excited and fast-speaking voice at the other end began, "Hi this is Karen, "You're not going to believe this. Are you sitting down?" she asked.

"No, but tell me anyway Karen," I said.

"Listen to this. I bought a swimwear magazine to look-over styles and the models and their poses. It was there I saw a swimwear advertisement announcing a search for new models for the *Ujena Swimwear* magazine. . I'm just wondering if you think I should send in that photo you liked so much." Before I could answer, she asked, "Do you see me getting called for an audition or a contract with them? Also, do you think the one you selected is good enough to send in to this magazine?"

"Karen as far as I'm concerned," I replied, "You have already been chosen from possibly hundreds of hopeful girls—especially if you use the picture that was in my vision."

"Are you serious?" she said, with a hint of disbelief in her voice. "You really see me getting called and modeling for this magazine?"

"What do I have to do to convince you that you will be modeling in that magazine; by the time their next issue hits the news stand. There is a reason why you just happened to find that particular magazine and, it's the same reason in fact as to why you had the pictures taken to begin with." I said, trying to reassure her. "I also know it was no coincidence that you came to me for a reading when you did."

"That must be true," Karen stated, "because really I could have easily gone to someone else, and they might not have seen the same destiny for me."

Feeling as though I still had some persuading to do, I offered my best advice. "Now, all you have to do Karen, is to start thinking positive. Visualize yourself in front of busy stage-sets with flashing cameras all about you. Start to imagine all the excitement that goes along with modeling—the fun, the travelling, the people, the way of life, the money for doing something you will love, So just go out and buy the champagne now—don't wait, just go out and buy it, as if you already got the stint with this Swim Wear Magazine' Keep it in your fridge, so it will be on hand for the big celebration!" Karen's favorite saying was, "Are you serious?" I remember pre-empting her question, laughing and saying, "And yes, I'm serious! Don't forget, I was also serious about having one of the first copies of the magazine."

"Oh for sure," she replied, "in fact, I'll get you a dozen of them if I get a job modeling for this Magazine."

We chatted a bit longer, and somehow we both could sense that something very exciting was about to happen—a chance in a lifetime really. I laughed in return and told Karen, "You can have the first copy of the magazine, because I would be more than honored to have any copy."

The next few months went flying by. One warm September day while vacationing in Vancouver British Columbia I

Chapter 10 • Once in a Lifetime

got a call from Karen on my cell phone while walking the oceanfront on the edge of the city. Her call was short, but it had the news I was waiting for.

"Hi, it's Karen. You were right! I was called by *Ujena Swimwear*. I had a stint with them last month, and I am in the latest issue just like you said. Can you believe it?" Her voice, as I remember it, was one of the most excited I had ever heard.

"I'm thrilled for you Karen. I want to hear all the details, and see the magazine. Why don't you meet me at my sister's house where I'm visiting right now? I know she would love to hear your story too."

"Oh perfect," she squealed, "Give me her address and I'll be there whatever time you say."

As Karen regaled us with the many behind-the-scenes stories and side-bars, My sister Julie and I sat in absolute awe, and especially so when Karen handed me the *Ujena* magazine that featured her pictures. The first photo was the exact one I had predicted. It not only seemed amazing to my sister, it seemed amazing to me as well.

The following year, I was in Palm Springs for the winter when I noticed a *Ujena* magazine laying upon a poolside table. It belonged to someone, but I was compelled to pick it up and flip through it anyway. I knew I was very likely to see a shot or two of Karen. And sure enough, there were actually several pictures of her and she looked fabulous. Not only that, she appeared just as she did in my vision!

By the time my vacation was over the following month, and I had gotten back to Vancouver, Karen was already booked for another reading at my sister's house where I was staying for a few days. It was not unlike any of her other readings. It was wonderful to sit and listen to such a happy, confident young woman, whose life was exciting, dynamic and adventurous all at the same time. Not to mention in such a short time.

"Who is Mark?" I asked. "Do you know a Mark?"

"Why?"

"I see you falling in love...a new chapter of your life is about to unfold."

"It is?"

"Yes, you're going to marry, have two children—a girl first is what I see, and—"

"Hold it , hold it! What about my career?"

"You will still be modeling my dear, don't worry. However, I also see you getting involved with your own business."

"My own business?" Karen exclaimed. "What kind of business?"

"I'm not sure, but you will have your own personal line of something."

"Could it be swimwear?"

"No, I don't see clothing." I said, with certainty in my voice. "I see you driving a red colored sport scar, a convertible, . I see you in a dizzying array of many more photo-shoots, in far away places, on white sandy untouched beaches. I see exotic locations in Spanish-speaking countries. That could mean anywhere from Spain to the Caribbean to South America.

"I can see that," Karen said, "I can actually see that too."

After the reading was over and we were making our way to the door, she reached into her tote bag and gave me a couple more of the magazines which featured her inside.

Chapter 10 • *Once in a Lifetime*

"I feel so good about my life right now, she panted, and I'm so thankful for you being in it, I hope we will always be friends"

As I gave her a hug and thanked her for her kind words I said, "You are just at the beginning Karen. Enjoy, and in particular, savor the ride for there is a lot more coming your way."

"The beginning?" she queried. "What do you mean exactly?"

"The beginning of the rest of your life."

"Hmmm...," she contemplated, with that same twinkle in her eye, "I'm going to sleep on that one"

Three months later we got together again to catch up on all the latest news with *Ujena Swimwear*. It was so much different now talking to Karen. Her confidence level was higher than ever before, and when she said things like, "I really feel I'm doing what I love, and what I should be doing in this life. She emanated a genuine sense of pride and accomplishment.

"I'm glad your loving what your doing Karen, because I see you modeling with this magazine for sometime—many years perhaps."

"You think so—for the same magazine? Wow! I am so happy with my life right now, it just couldn't be better, and just to know that you see me working for them for many years, all of this really is a dream coming true!"

"I thought you would be getting used to it by now Karen," I said joking. As I closed the door behind her, I could hear her cell phone ringing and thought to myself, *now that is one busy girl*.

It wasn't long after this that Karen called again saying she wanted to come by for another reading. Needless to say, I was looking forward to it as much as she was and we quickly made arrangements. It was another fascinating reading, one that held more excitement, adventure, and life changing, love-encompassing dynamics.

I found Karen was always easy to read, and as the years went by we became closer as friends. Karen did finally meet and fall madly in love with the man of her dreams, and she brought him to meet me shortly thereafter. I liked him right from the start and, yes, his name was Mark! He had good aura, great energy, and was very polite and genuinely thoughtful. He was tall with a slim, athletic build and sported thick wavy blonde hair. All-in-all, a very handsome guy. All I kept thinking was, *They sure will have good-looking children!* His personality was exactly like the man I described in her previous readings—from his smile, to the shoes he was wearing. Karen felt her life was about to move on to another chapter when we talked about her expecting her first child. She told me how her children would be the first and foremost important thing in her life and I ventured to say as I had many times before, "Karen you will always be a model for as long as you want to. Children will never interfere with that in any way."

"I know that too, and that's why I want to start my family while I'm young."

Karen began traveling the globe extensively with her modeling career in full-swing. She continued doing so right up until her first was born. Then, as soon as the kids were at walking-age they had a nanny on-board. Between her husband Mark and her nanny, Karen managed to not only carry on modeling, but she struck gold again—she began building an empire in the soap business. In one of her readings, I had told her that I could see her own business being very successful and, that it would one day be huge. It would be just one of many accomplishments to come.

Chapter 10 • Once in a Lifetime

The following year the soap business started to go through the roof. She found a distributor who taught her how to launch this new scent, and how to take it to market. The brand name was finally decided on—for this beautiful line of soaps— *LUSH*. She opened up the first store in Hawaii and the second and third and forth in other parts of the world. There are now over six hundred of these unique *LUSH* boutiques globally.

Karen is now forty-two years old. She has been modeling steady for over twenty years, and she is still doing photo-shoots for swimwear magazines. She still goes to tropical locales like Mexico, and other places in the sun for on-location work. She is the mom of two lovely children, one a beautiful girl who looks a lot like her mom and, her son who is just adorable and looks just like Mark. She last phoned me from Paris, where she was spending the winter with her family. She had just launched her own line of perfume in the UK and wanted to tell me all about it. I always love hearing from her, because there is never a dull moment—always something new in the making. I feel privileged not only knowing Karen, but also for having generous gifts of *LUSH* products delivered to my door when I least expect it.

Chapter 11

ANGEL INTERVENTION

"What do you mean, I will read the past?" I said, in complete disbelief after hearing these words whispered in my ears.

These were some of the words that were blurting out of my mouth to my angels and spirit guides that day. I even found myself trying to figure out a way in which I could get out of reading this particular client, for no other reason except that I couldn't pick up anything she didn't already know. I knew she would not be happy having a reading that only told her about her past, she wanted to know about her future, like most people do. It was the first time in all my years of reading clients, that I was actually caught in a situation that left me frozen with apprehension...

It happened sometime in the early eighties. I had a cozy brightly decorated little room set up in my home, where I felt the most comfortable reading. It was a Saturday morning, just after breakfast when the phone rang.

A friendly female voice began inquiring as to my services and wanted to schedule appointments for some readings. Usually I am busy catching up on baking, canning, or gardening and I don't read on the weekends, but this

Chapter 11 • *Angel Intervention*

woman's voice sounded pretty convincing, so I decided to postpone the chores for the time being.

"I would like to make four appointments for tea-cup readings," the sweet voice stated at the other end of the line. "I know its short notice, but not very often all of us four sisters get together. I thought it might be a fun thing to do," she added convincingly.

"How does 10:30 sound?" I asked.

"Oh, that will work wonderfully," she said, with a hint of excitement. "What is your address?"

I got her name and then gave out my address. Giving her the directions, she quickly said, "I know exactly where you live, I will see you at 10:30 if that's okay for you."

It seemed like only minutes later when I heard a ring at my door, and these four lovely women whom I had never seen before were introducing themselves and taking off their coats, They kicked their shoes aside in such a fashion as to suggest they were going to be staying for a while. I am one of the worst people when it comes to remembering names, but for some reason I spent extra effort getting their names straight. I purposely made a mental note association with something that rhymed with their name.

When I sat down with them for the first few minutes while they enjoyed their cup of tea, I picked up some fragmented energy from one of the sisters—the one who was sitting beside me, to my right. She hardly spoke a word and seemed to be lost in another world all of her own. Her sisters were doing all the talking while she just smiled as if simultaneously listening to another conversation somewhere else. The energy I was picking up from her was like a fog, and something about her aura was telling me I wouldn't have the easiest time reading her. This fog bothered me. I continued to wonder why her three sisters were lit up like neon at night as I contemplated the contrasts before me. I knew these three would be very easy to read as their energy was open and unguarded. Ready, in all likelihood, to be read like a book. I didn't say anything but I knew that something wasn't quite right with Annie, the quiet one, and I wasn't looking forward to reading her. By the time they all finished their tea, it was time to get started reading their tea-cups—which was their choice, as apposed to Tarot cards.

I read them one by one leaving Annie until last. I found myself wondering why I would do that—why wouldn't I take her in the middle somewhere as I would normally do when a little group came together. This was making me somewhat edgy and even a little nervous since I knew she really wanted to be read and I didn't want to disappoint her and say something like, "I'm sorry but... I just can't read you." So, just before it was her turn, I politely asked them, "Would you ladies excuse me for a few minutes while I take a breather?"

They smiled at me and offered, "Of course, take as long as you need, you must be getting exhausted."

"No, I'm not exhausted yet," I replied, "but I will take five minutes if you don't mind."

I casually walked into the other room and took a long and deep breath. I knew that I was faced with a situation I hadn't experienced before, and that I would have to summon my Angels for assistance. I sat in my favourite meditation chair facing the seventy acres of pasture out my sunroom window and went into a meditation state, closing my eyes and asking spirit, angels and spirit guides for all the help they could give. My prayer was simply, "I ask you at this time dear angels and spirit if you can help me

Chapter 11 • Angel Intervention

with my reading I am about to give.. I need your messages loud and clear... Please help me read her—give me the messages I need." My five minutes had just elapsed when, suddenly, I heard the message. It was whispered in my ear and it seemed as if my angel was standing there in the room beside me. It was quite incredible! The words were very clear and to the point.

"You will see her past." "You will read her past"

"What do you mean, I will see her past? She is here to learn about her *future*. I whispered. Seconds later, the message had resonated enough in me to give me the confidence I was going to need.

Everything seemed clear. I opened my eyes and was ready to get on my feet, when I heard the faint but firm, "Go read Annie, you will be fine." The voice which I felt was that of my Angel, was almost laughing now. "You will be fine," was repeated again.

And, on that positive note, I did a pirouette onto my feet as if someone had spun me around like a top. I closed my hands and raised them upwards saying, "Thank-you my dear Angel." I took another long and deep breath, this time one of relief. I was ready now for Annie, and I found myself almost excited to know that I was going to be able to give her a good reading. Whatever was going to come through was going to come through, and there would be nothing I could do about it...and I would be fine... According to my angels and guides that is...

Just before going around the corner to the room where I had left the four sisters sitting drinking their tea, I heard one of them say to the others, "She saw tears around me. I wonder *who* is crying..."

"Yes, she saw tears around me as well," another sister commented. They were comparing notes, as anyone would.

"Well Annie," I said smiling, as I let my presence be known, "the moment you've been waiting for."

Picking up her tea-cup, she jumped up from her chair and followed me into the reading room, asking politely, "Do you mind if I just have a half hour reading today. We're running a bit late, and we need to do some shopping before returning home. We have a bit of a drive ahead of us."

"Oh, of course, Annie." I answered, not unhappy with the request. *My angels really were working with me on this one,* I thought to myself. Thanking them under my breath, we sat down upon the comfy chairs facing the view of wild yellow daisies that blanket the fields behind our house every spring.

"This is going to be so much fun!" she said as she rubbed her hands together. Annie handed me her tea-cup. I turned it over gently before turning it around three times.

Instantly I said, "You never ask for anything except health, happiness and family." Smiling and looking into her eyes, I continued with, "You have a wonderful son, who is going to be going through a big change very soon. I feel your husband was very ill and has recently passed away. You were a caregiver for many years before he passed. He was a great man who suffered a lot, and died far too young."

Annie nodded and said, "Yes, he had many health problems due to diabetes."

I cleared my throat and took a deep breath, looking straight into her eyes and, trying to get a vision of her future—any vision—but the fog I was picking up earlier came through once again. This time however, it was much

Chapter 11 • Angel Intervention

thicker. The fog was floating just above her head, like a cloud. By now I was getting worried that I would have to tell her what the problem was but as she sat quietly there I suddenly had a very clear vision of her past. Her childhood came through as if she were living it at that very moment!

"I see you as a young girl, working a farm on the prairies. You had lots of cows and chickens. You loved the farm. The farm house is still there. You grew up in a hurry—not much time for play. You had a bad fall in the barn and injured your shoulder. You married your first love. Your dad was your idol growing up. You lost him when you were very young." This reading, all about her past as the angels had said it would be, went on and on—for the half hour and then some. When she paid me I folded the money up and tucked it back into her pocket telling her, "I don't want to take your money for telling you everything you already know!"

"But, I want to pay you," she insisted, pulling the money from her pocket and trying again to give it to me.

"No, I will not hear of it. I'm serious Annie. Please, just keep your money and I will feel a lot better."

"Well okay, but only this once; I don't like getting something for nothing. I have always paid my way through life."

"Of course you have Annie, but this is different."

As I helped them all with their coats, I knew that there was a significant reason why I could not see anything in Annie's future. It bothered me to the point where it was agitating. We said our goodbyes with a hug and I wished the four of them well. As I stood in the driveway watching their big Chrysler Imperial pull out, I knew in my heart—and with every cell in my body—that I would not be seeing Annie again. It was something that was quite inexplicable and I wondered if she had any premonitions or feelings about her life as many people do.

It wasn't two weeks later when I got another phone call from Dorothy, the outgoing sister that I read first that day. I was still in my pajamas making a pot of coffee for my husband when the phone rang. Before answering it, I had a very strong feeling that I would hear the voice of one of the sisters on the other end of the line. I picked the phone up only to hear a faint, sad, and unrecognizable voice that was obviously stuffed up from crying.

"Hello, this is Dorothy, the woman who you read along with my sisters a couple of weeks ago. I have some very sad news to tell you". Before I could say anything, she carried on in a sinking voice, "Do you remember my sister Annie, the one you read last?"

"Of course I do." I said as I swallowed the lump in my throat. Standing there shaking, and feeling sick to my stomach, like I do when I get upsetting and shocking news. I tried to find some comforting words, and stay calm at the same time. "I'm so sorry Dorothy, I'm just so sorry. She was a lovely woman, I'm sure you're all going to miss her terribly." I didn't know what else to say.

" I also wanted to tell you what happened the day we left your house. Do you have a minute?"

"Absolutely Dorothy, go ahead." I answered as I sat down on the nearest chair feeling it had to be an interesting story.

"Well," she started, "when we left your house that day, we were all talking about our readings. How one of us was moving, and getting a new red car, etc. And then we noticed that Annie was quiet, not saying a word, and when we asked what was wrong she told us very sadly, 'Well all

Chapter 11 • Angel Intervention

of you had a reading about the nice things that are going to happen, and all she read for me was my past. I wanted to know about my future, so I'm just disappointed, that's all.' We all felt bad for her, but didn't know exactly what to say at the time. So, we finally just told her that sometimes certain people are harder to read."

"Thank you for comforting her with those words because they are very true." I replied.

What Dorothy said next I have never forgotten. "We just wanted you to know that we appreciate the fact that you didn't lie or make up anything for her future—just to make her happy. You told it like you saw it, genuinely. You didn't see any future, and never told her one single thing about her future. The tears you saw in our cups were the tears we are still shedding for our dear sister."

Thinking of Annie's loss caused me a near loss for words. "Well I would never distort or fabricate, I can tell you that much Dorothy. I only say something if I see it, and if I don't see it, I just can't make things up. But thank you so much for your kind words. I really appreciate your phone call, especially at a time like this. You all must be going through a very stressful time." We chatted a few minutes more, and before hanging up I said, "You take care of yourself and your sisters, and do keep in touch—feel free to call me whenever you like if you need someone to talk to."

"Thanks Mary. We are happy to have met you and we will definitely keep in touch."

After hanging up the phone, I took a deep breath. Knowing why I didn't see any future for Annie, and why I seen such grey dark aura around her. I also realized that if it were to happen again—which I was sure it would—I wouldn't be intimidated by it. If I were to get messages from the past instead of the future, I would deal with it in terms of the understanding I now have. I knew as well that if a clear vision of fog, just like the sky before a thunder storm, hovering above, or around, someone, it may very likely mean they are here for a short time.

Several weeks went by and for some reason one particular day I couldn't seem to get Annie and her sudden death off my mind. I sat for the longest time out in my rose garden, sipping tea, trying to read. Yet the events of what had happened two weeks earlier with Annie seemed to haunt me all day long. The extraordinary way in which I hadn't picked up anything for her future, the way my angels had given me her past instead, and, just the way I didn't want to read her until last. I didn't know if it was normal having someone I had only just met have such an enormous impact on me. Just as I was gazing up to the sky, my phone rang. I made a mad dash into the house to get the call. Immediately, I began wondering if this phone call was why I had been thinking about Annie all day long.

"Hello Mary, this is Dorothy again. Remember us, the sisters you read."

"Hi, Dorothy. I've been thinking about you ladies all day long."

"Well when I tell you what happened today, you will know why you were probably thinking of us today. It was unnerving and unbelievable, yet beautiful at the same time—I have to see you because what I have to show you is going to shock you, as it did us!"

"You've got my curiosity now Dorothy, so by all means, come over right away if you like."

"Great!" Dorothy said, sounding upbeat. "I'll see you within a half hour."

Hanging up, I put my hand to my chin, trying to figure

Chapter 11 • *Angel Intervention*

out what this shocking thing could possibly be. Impatiently, I waited for her to arrive. I kept thinking how odd it was that I was thinking of Annie all day long—someone I hardly knew. And then, the phone call from her sister afterwards. I was fairly well convinced that it had to be something to do with Annie. I finished my tea, and got ready to greet Dorothy at the door.

Minutes later the doorbell rang. She stood in the doorway with a tea-cup in two pieces. For a second I thought my eyes were playing tricks on me. The beautiful fine china tea-cup was literally in two halves—one half with the handle still attached which she was holding along with the other half which sat cradled in the palm of her other hand. She looked at me with tears in her eyes. We were both speechless for a fleeting moment, and then I invited her in. I wanted to hear how and when this cup broke into two pieces as though someone had cut through it with a diamond-bladed knife. I knew instantly that something quite miraculous had just happened and that it had much to do with Annie.

"Please come in and make yourself comfortable Dorothy."

As she followed me upstairs, gently holding the once perfect tea-cup in her hands, she told me, "You won't believe what happened today."

"Tell me, tell me!" I replied, gingerly taking the two pieces of this beautiful tea-cup from her.

After taking a deep breath, exhaling steadily and slowly, and then taking off her coat, she finally said, "It was only an hour ago and, I must tell you, we are all still in a tremendous state of shock." "Maybe you can explain why' and what' it means."

" Go ahead, tell me what happened," I said, with curiosity racing through me.

"Well," she started, looking like she had just seen a ghost, "my sisters and I got together today at my home. We were nicely having a nice hot cup of tea and reminiscing about Annie when one of us said, 'I wonder if we will ever get any messages from her, or if she can hear us talking, and wouldn't it be nice if she was here with us enjoying this tea time... and just mere seconds later, this tea-cup that I had been drinking from, was sitting in it's saucer empty, started to tremble and vibrate, just like it was dancing, and we all watched in disbelief, for the few seconds, and then it just broke right in two, just as you see it". I handed Dorothy the box of Kleenex as she broke down and cried just talking about how uncanny and unbelievable this was.

Shaking my head in amazement, and still holding the two pieces of the cup in my hands I said, "I believe that Annie was trying to tell you sisters that she is still around you in spirit, and wants you to talk to her whenever you like because she doesn't miss a thing"

As Dorothy was wiping away her tears she said, "You know, I never really thought too much about the spirits before, but now that this has happened to us, right in front of us—we all witnessed such a beautiful thing—it would be hard for any of us not to believe."

Handing Dorothy back the broken tea-cup, and still shaking my head in disbelief, I said, "She will continue to communicate with you, especially when you are all together at tea time"

"I know one thing for sure," she offered with a very peaceful smile.

"What's that Dorothy?" almost knowing what she was going to say.

Chapter 11 • Angel Intervention

"We will always remember Annie at tea time!"

"Yes," I agreed, "and I will never look at a tea-cup quite the same"

The gift of love cannot be held in your hand, for it is something only held in your heart.

~Unknown

Chapter 12

MIRACLES REALLY DO HAPPEN

Sometimes in life we hear those beautiful love stories of how couples meet there loved ones. You have to admit, some of them are so romantic you just know they would make a good movie for the big screen, or a novel that would make the *New York Times* best-sellers list. This is one of those exciting love stories that I predicted in the mid-eighties—when I was still trying to get my name established as an intuitive-reader in the Okanagan Valley in southern British Columbia.

I was just coming in, through the front door of my house after a busy day at a beauty salon in Vernon. I was on my way to the fridge when I noticed my answering machine flashing away. I pressed 'play' and continued to go about pouring myself a cold drink. All the messages were from friends or family and clients whose names I was familiar with, until a very soft, unknown voice came on asking to book an appointment. Instantly I felt a connection to his voice—like I had heard it before. I quickly reached for my pen, jotted down his name and number, and called him. It was then I realized that I hadn't ever heard his voice before—he was indeed a perfect stranger.

Chapter 12 • *Miracles Really Do Happen*

"Hi Bill, This is Mary returning your call. I got your message."

"Hi there, Thanks for calling back so quickly. I would love to come for a reading—when is a good time for you?"

"Well this is your lucky day. I happen to have an opening at two tomorrow, so if you would like to come by at that time I—"

"That will be perfect! How do I find you?" He seemed quite excited, unless of course it was his normal demeanor I thought to myself. I gave him directions with which he said he'd make a 'mental map.' "Thank you so much, I will see you tomorrow at two."

As I hung up the phone I stared at it for a moment or two thinking to myself, *this man is going to have a story to tell*.

The next day, I picked a gorgeous bouquet of gladiolas and baby's breath from the garden, and had my reading room emanating the sweet spring scent of a florist's shop. I lit my votive candles and scattered some of my feathers and precious stones around the reading table and, by two o'clock on the nose, I heard the door bell ring. Seconds later, he was in my foyer introducing himself as Bill, and telling me how he had heard about me by eaves-dropping on some women sitting at the food fair in the shopping-mall. I found that quite amusing knowing how noisy the food fair is at the best of times, and we chuckled over that as I led him to my reading room.

"It seems as though I've met you before" I said as I led him up the staircase to the reading room.

"No I don't think so" he laughed "Because I live in Vancouver, I am just up here for the weekend"

"Do you read tarot cards?" he asked.

"Yes, and I also read tea leaves. Why do you ask?"

"Well if you don't mind, I would prefer a teacup reading verses cards, because I like the energy better."

"Perfect. I actually like the teacups over the cards myself as well," I agreed. As I was preparing his cup of tea, I started picking up all kinds of things. It seemed crazy at the moment, but none-the-less I wanted to tell him everything that was coming through. Things began to blurt out of my mouth from out of seemingly nowhere.

"I see big changes around you. You will be starting over."

He shook his head and I caught a glare in his eye. "I can't see that, because I've already started over. I can't start all over *again*."

Almost ignoring his statement, I said, "Oh yes. You *will* be starting over, again I can assure you of that."

Shaking his head and taking a deep breath like it was his last he said, "Okay, go on."

By now he was drinking his tea at an ever-faster rate, and then it was gone. I told him, "I see you going to Mexico."

"To Mexico?" he exclaimed, looking astonished. "I won't be going to Mexico, or anywhere else for that matter. I'm broke...I have no money—especially for travel, so I can't see it happening."

Sidetracking his monetary concerns, I went on to reveal to him a vision that was as clear as watching a movie on television. "I see a new love around you. She is a brunette with olive skin, Spanish-speaking. She lives in Mexico."

Appearing restless and fidgeting about in his seat, Bill handed me the tea-cup. "Uh, but...I'm living with a girl who is Scandinavian. She is blonde and she doesn't speak any Spanish. I can't see any of this, but obviously you do," he continued with a hint of intrigue in his voice.

Chapter 12 • *Miracles Really Do Happen*

"I'm sorry Bill, but the girl you are involved with now is not going to be in your life for long."

"But...what happens to her—I've been with her for two years now."

"That I'm afraid, is up to you and the universe. She will not be in your life much longer. I'm seeing three months or less, as the time-line for the end of this relationship."

By the time we got around to the teacup a half-hour had somehow slipped by. Suddenly, I had a sense of Bill's working environment. "I see you working away in a place where there are mountains of paper all about, stacks and stacks of paper. And, a chemical or ink-like smell in the air., like at a laundry matt with that chemical smell".. Not a healthy place...I'm picking up an ambiance of stress and anxiety." But the smell' is something terrible I said, as I held my nose like I could smell it in my house.

"You've sure nailed that one on the head!" Bill replied, "I work at the *Vancouver Sun* newspaper."

"I'm growing weary of the toxic work environment. Do you see me leaving there anytime soon?"

Shaking my head and looking straight into his eyes I said, "I see you staying there. I don't see you leaving—not in the near future at least. So, you may as well make the best of it."

"Dag-nam it!" he said with disappointment. "I *was* contemplating looking for another job."

Before he could ask another question I blurted out a name that had rushed to me. "Who is Carmel?"

Rubbing his forehead as if searching his memory, he replied, "I don't know anyone with that name."

"Well, I'm picking up that name very clearly, but it is

only part of her whole name." At that moment I felt like I was in a trance—somewhere else it seemed. I was fixated upon this woman who was coming through so strong and yet from a considerable distance. It was unbelievable. As I relayed these messages to Bill he appeared mesmerized by the whole experience and was speechless through most of his reading in worry of interrupting its course.

"Maybe it is Carmel California," Bill finally said, still racking his memory as to who Carmel could be.

"No it has nothing to do with Carmel California, it is not a place, it's a person. But, it is only part of the girl's name. You will meet her very soon. And, I also see two little children." I said, grinning.

"Oh yes, that is true. I have two children; two beautiful girls."

Tilting my head down and looking over the top of my reading glasses, I looked Bill square in the eye and told him, "No Bill, these children are going to be with your *new* wife—you will have two more children; a boy first, and then a girl."

Laughing out loud, he cried out, "No, no, that is impossible—I had a vasectomy thirteen years ago."

I smiled and said, "You may have had a vasectomy, but you will father two more of your very own children. I see them with Spanish names in fact! The boy will be named after a grandfather or some other relation from Mexico."

At this point Bill was upset and appeared ready to walk out the door. I had the distinct feeling he was thinking I was the worst psychic he had ever seen in his life. I didn't let this bother me, and continued on to say, "She is definitely in Mexico. And, she is of Spanish decent. You will be learning the Spanish language, and she in turn will learn

Chapter 12 • *Miracles Really Do Happen*

English for you. She speaks some English already, but just enough to get by with."

Bill got up and stretched his legs and asked if he could have a drink of water. I got up and reached for the glass pitcher of ice-water I had upon the credenza. Bill thirstily drank back half the glass before sitting again and we continued. While sipping away the remainder of his drink he declared, "I'm in total shock. I don't really know what to believe. I'm really confused over the 'two more kids,' you see. I only know that it is quite impossible because I've been fixed—no sperm, no children!"

Smiling and amused by it myself, I replied in my usual humorous voice, "I don't care if you've been fixed with cement, you will get this wonderful woman Carmel pregnant and, you will be a daddy once again!"

Shaking his head again, and finding me not the least bit humorous he said, "Maybe this girl that I'm supposed to meet already has two kids!"

"No Bill," I answered as I continued to look into his eyes, "she is single, she's never been married and she has no children."

Almost choking on his second glass of water he argued his point, "But that's impossible, I don't have any available 'swimmers,' since my vasectomy that is."

Ignoring his words, and chuckling at his choice of words, I informed him further. "You will get married there, in Mexico."

"You actually see me getting married again...because I swore I never would."

"I sure do," I assured him with excitement, "In fact Bill, I can see you sending me an invitation to your wedding in Mexico! I see Carmel being in her late twenties" "She has strong family ties... she has a good job; "A charming and captivating personality.. "She is very beautiful with long dark hair". "Oh, and she laughs a lot" "And Bill,... She will fall in love with you at first sight! "You'll meet her while on vacation...I see a cruise ship" "You must book with a cruise-line within the next three months."

As I was picking up these finer details and passing them along to Bill, he began scribbling them down upon his notepad fast and furious as to not forget one single word. With a weight of under-riding sadness in his voice, he wiped his brow and asked me, "But what am I suppose to do about the girl I'm with now—I don't like hurting people and, besides, she is a very nice person, undeserving of any such scenarios,... and—

Shaking my head sympathetically I offered some supportive words. "Bill, when destiny and the universe are working in tune with one another, and you are open to change, your life will change. . Just don't wait too long—Carmel is waiting for you."

"Wow. You've got me infatuated with this."

"This woman will leave her country for you Bill! She will also leave her family and friends behind. She will give up her career as a secretary, and be a full-time mom. That's how much she will love you!"

Looking like he had just seen a ghost, he asked, "You actually see this?"

"Bill, my vision of this is so intense and so clear that it's like watching a love story at a movie theatre."

Looking over his notes, which he could hardly read, he shakily wiped his brow again from sheer anxiety and announced, "I have another question for you."

"Fire away Bill, that's what I'm here for."

Chapter 12 • Miracles Really Do Happen

He seemed to have a thousand questions on his mind, and then he settled in with the first one. "Where do you see me living?"

"On the coast, You will build this woman a dream house, and will raise your children in this home"

After a dozen or more questions about the new girl whom he was going to meet in Mexico, he began to deliberate and reason out loud, "I can't just go gallivanting off to Mexico on the chance that you've seen a girl that might be there and that I might also meet."

"No, but when you say the word can't or might, you send negative intonations to your subconscious mind and, consequently, detract from your positive energy—energy you are going to need in order to attract a positive response. You need to change your thought process and start saying to yourself 'I am going to go on a trip, because I am going to meet the girl of my dreams. And, I will marry her!'"

Smiling, he appeared more relaxed now. "Okay, I'm going to do that from today onwards, because deep down I know your right. As you say, I just have to change my *way* of thinking and be more positive."

"Very good," I laughed, "you're a fast learner."

"Yah, I might be a fast learner alright, but I wish I didn't have to hurt the girl I am with now."

"Look at it this way Bill," I reasoned, as I got up from my chair, "you will be setting her free so that she too can find the love of her life."

Smiling once again and feeling more confident of me and himself, he replied, "I will have to remember that. Those are very philosophical words."

What started out to be an hour reading, turned out to be just over two. Neither one of us realized how much time had actually passed. By the time it was over, Bill made sure he had my phone number tucked away in his pocket. He left excitedly, forgetting his pen, jacket, and sunglasses. If that wasn't enough, he almost tripped over the threshold on his way out the door!

It was about two weeks later when, out working in my flower beds, I heard the phone ring. I had been thinking about Bill here and there throughout the day, and wasn't surprised when I heard the voice at the other end saying, "Do you remember me? I'm the guy you told would be meeting a woman in Mexico."

Knowing the voice instantly, I said, "Yes, I sure do! What's happening?"

"Well, I've been doing a lot of thinking about my reading, and I don't know if I have the nerves—or the funds—to do what you said. I just can't risk taking the chance that it might not happen."

Listening to this poor man trying to think up excuses of why he couldn't go was sad to hear. I knew that if he didn't go, he would never meet the woman I saw him with. I almost scolded him into changing his mind, by saying, "Bill, listen to me. Are you happy right now?"

"Well, no, not exactly."

"Would you like to be happier than you have ever been?"

"Yes...I cannot lie. Of course I would."

"Then *believe* in your answer Bill," I said, with a hint of lecturing tone in my voice. "You have to start believing in yourself. Have the confidence that you *can* and *will* make this happen. If you follow your heart, keep open to change, think positive, and believe in your destiny, it *will* all happen. It's your fate Bill." Before he could articulate an answer to my lecturing words, I added, "Do you remember me saying, "We all have the power to change our destiny?"

Chapter 12 • *Miracles Really Do Happen*

"I do remember. In fact I wrote it down as you were saying it!"

"Well then. Stay positive and visualize only positive thoughts. Whenever you start having negative thoughts, just replace the thought with something that you want to see happen that is beautiful and positive! For instance," I continued with a big smile, "start visualizing that you have already met this beautiful woman and, what she will feel like when you touch and embrace her for the first time. Imagine to yourself how romantic it will be when she talks to you in Spanish. I know you are still skeptical and, no doubt a little unconvinced of my skills as a psychic—"

Before I could finish, Bill came alive and interjected. He explained, "You don't know how much I want to believe you, but... well...it's just the bit about the 'kids' and to tell you the truth, I feel that most of my reading, really, was kinda far-fetched."

"I know," I answered. "That it is over-whelming to you now is only normal. But, I have seen how it goes many times before. It won't be long before you'll be telling me your love story, and all the details of how you met this beautiful Spanish woman."

At that, we said our goodbyes and as I hung up the phone, I was determined to keep my hopes up for Bill. Hope that he would, at the end of the day, have trust in his heart.

Several weeks passed before I heard from him again. AIt was a phone-call that I had felt was coming any day and one that I could feel was going to deliver some positive and happy news. "Hi Mary, It's Bill—the guy you think should be going to Mexico."

"How is everything going now Bill?" I asked with enthusiasm.

"Well, I thought you would like to know that I did it!"

"Really?" I said, wondering exactly what it was that he did.

"Yes, I broke up with my girlfriend and, luckily, we are still friends. And guess what else?" he asked. But before I could guess, he answered himself, "I'm all booked with *Club Med* for a cruise—how do you like that?"

"I'm so excited for you Bill! Sounds like you didn't forget what I had said about your timing, how very important it is I mean."

He laughed and announced, "If all this does actually come true, you will be getting the first invitation to the wedding!"

"Thank-you Bill, but I haven't been too much of a fan of Mexico—maybe I'll wait until your wedding in Canada."

After listening to some further details of Bill's cruise-vacation package, he wished me all the best and promised he would call the day he returned home. We were just about to say goodbye when he suddenly changed his tone of voice to one of sheer urgency, if not quite panic. He quickly asked what could only be considered a crucial question, "One last thing I want to ask you. *Where*, in Mexico is this Senorita?"

I listened for a moment, and all of a sudden I could hear Spanish music with a Mariachi Band and the word Puerto Vallarta came to me. The words were no sooner on the tip of my tongue when I blurted it out. "You will find yourself in a place called Puerto Vallarta, but I don't know the exact spot" but you will find her there while she is also on vacation"

With excitement in his voice, as if he had just answered the million-dollar-question, he cried out, I've always wanted to go there. So now I at least know where I'm going."

Chapter 12 • *Miracles Really Do Happen*

I laughed and told Bill, "Have the time of your life, because it will never be the same once you come back."

"I know you go away for the winter but I would like to get in touch with you as soon as I get back—to let you know how it all went. What number, or numbers, can I reach you at?"

It was about three weeks later when the phone rang at my parent's home where I was spending a week before heading to Palm Springs for the winter. When my mom called me to the phone she had it covered with her hand. "It's a man," she whispered. She handed it to me with a curious eye, wondering who on earth would be calling me at her number. The normal chatter around the dinner table went perfectly silent the moment I began talking. Addressing the caller as Bill had obviously piqued everyone's curiosity. Their ears really perked up when, a couple of minutes later, I said, "Why don't you come over to my parent's house so you can tell us all about this incredible love story. It's already sounding too beautiful not to share!"

He had, of course, the news that I was expecting. His voice was so excited and he was talking so fast that he had trouble speaking. "You were right! You were right! Her name is Carmelita. You said that Carmel was part of her name! You won't believe the story of how we met. I have to see you—*when* can I see you? You are going to be amazed. For me, I was infatuated—it was like a miracle."

I could tell he was on cloud-nine to say the least, and even though my house was full of Christmas visitors at the time, I figured that they too would enjoy hearing the intriguing details behind this beautiful love story. At that, I invited Bill over to join in all the Christmas spirit at my parent's home in North Vancouver.

After introductions and a fresh round of drinks we all

waited in anticipation. Everyone was sitting comfortably, yakking away having a glass of my dad's homemade wine when Bill announced that he was ready to tell us his dramatic love story. We quieted down so he could start. Everyone's eyes were on his.

"Well first, a little background. I'm a client of Mary's—make that a very happy client of Mary's! I'm only too happy to share with you what just happened to me in Mexico. All of this—all of what happened to me—Mary predicted. After you hear my story, I'm sure you'll probably all end up agreeing with me that miracles really *can* happen.

As you probably all know by now I had a reading by Mary three months ago, and she told me I was going to Mexico, and would meet the woman I would fall in love with and marry, she had given me the letters C..A.. R..M..E..L.. and told me they were part of her name—Well to make a long story short, she was only three letters shy of her complete first name! I found that quite astonishing. While I was aboard my ship, I had told a few people that I was only on the cruise, because a psychic reader told me I was to go on a trip to Mexico and meet the love of my life and, believe it or not, I met her on the very first day of my trip! I was sitting with friends in an enchanting patio-styled Restaurant shortly after we got into the port of Puerto Vallarta when I noticed this beautiful looking girl having a drink with another girl, and every time I looked her way, I noticed she was looking at me. Our eyes kept making contact! I was captivated by her apparent charm and warm smile the very second I set my eyes on her. Naturally, I went over to her table and invited them both to sit with us. They accepted the invitation without any hesitation, however it was immediately apparent to all that we had a problem. They couldn't speak much, if any, English and of course we couldn't speak much Spanish. Nonetheless, we

Chapter 12 • *Miracles Really Do Happen*

gallantly pulled up some chairs and spoke with our hands and our expressions. The girls introduced themselves as sisters, Carmelita and Chickie, when I heard her name "Carmelita" I just about fainted, I knew that moment that this was the girl I was going to marry, not only because her name was Carmelita, but because when I grasped her hand upon introductions, there was an energy like I had never felt before, it traveled right through to my spine. I was mesmerized and dazed. She was the exact description of how Mary had described her; long dark hair, an oval face, medium build five-foot-four with an infectious laugh, and an unforgettable smile."

At this point, Bill had the entire room captivated, and even my dad sat in his easy chair listening carefully as not to miss a single detail. Bill went on with his story, like he was the major part in a movie.

"After the group of us drank and enjoyed a lovely Mexican dinner and dancing, I was already feeling like this was the beginning of the rest of my life! This went on every day for one week, and every night we dined and danced and held each other close knowing that soon our holiday would have to come to an end. I thought that by dancing the nights away I could at least hold Carmelita close to me and feel the energy between us. And it was this closeness that was responsible for a touching moment that I don't think I will ever forget. During one of these beautiful slow waltzes, mid-song, or so, I felt a teardrop upon my shoulder where she was resting her head. I looked at her intently and motioned with my hands, attempting to convey the question, 'What's wrong—why are you crying?' With tears in her eyes she pointed to the big cruise ship which was clearly within view, docked in the harbor. I likely appeared somewhat confused but knew instinctively what she was trying to tell me. As she was circling her watch face with her finger, trying to make herself understood, my heart sank. I knew then exactly what she meant; our time together was about to expire. When her finger stopped at 8 o'clock, she pointed again to the ship, then to herself, saying very clearly, 'Me, Mexico City.' Just thinking about what was on Carmelita's mind sent waves of anxiety through me. I got the picture loud and clear. This beautiful and sincere woman I had only just met a week earlier, was leaving at eight the very next morning to go home where she lived. With an attempt to act as though it was nothing to cry about, I smiled and looked into her eyes. I then circled the face of my own watch just as she had done with hers, and stopped at the same hour—8 o'clock. I pointed to the same cruise ship, then to myself and her, and said 'Mexico City.' Understanding my rudimentary attempt at sign language she shook her head with tears still in her eyes. She said only one word, and it was a word that she knew how to say very well. 'NO!' boomed out of her, washing over me and the immediate area. She pointed to me simultaneously, and I knew right then and there I was not going back to Mexico City with her.

"My heart sank further, possibly even to my knees. We were both in a sad state of affairs and we both knew it. My vacation was only one week in the making, and the girl I had just fallen in love with, was leaving. All I kept thinking was, *This can't be happening. Mary didn't mention this as part of the equation.* At the moment I found myself not caring about anything except the immediate situation with Carmelita. I didn't want to let her go.

"I started to panic—my knees began feeling kinda' shaky. Then a peculiar sensation came over me. I remembered how beautiful the sunrises were in Mexico! So, we ended up just holding hands and walking the beaches all night long. We held each other, hugged, kissed, cried,

Chapter 12 • *Miracles Really Do Happen*

laughed and wiped away each others tears. We both knew we had fallen in love with each other at first sight as they say. It was a magical and unforgettable week. Both of us seemed to know in our hearts and in the deep recesses of our minds that this encounter was our shared destiny. Carmelita didn't want to leave me, but she realized she had to return home with her sister, not to mention getting back to her awaiting legal secretary job. Waiting for her to get ready to leave was the longest hours of my life actually. We connected again for breakfast with the same energy as all week long. Of course, we were still trying to communicate the best and only way we could, using improvised sign language and arbitrary words at random. We did our best and, for the most part, we understood each other. We had a few hours more. Before her ship disembarked for Mexico City, Carmelita made it known that she wanted to translate something to me."

By now all my family was interjecting with a flurry of questions, "What was the translated message?"

"What did you do when she departed Bill?"

"When are you going to go back to Mexico City?" Bill continued telling his story with a twinkle in his eyes.

"We're now at the most unbelievable part of the whole story and, it unfolded like a true miracle. Carmelita beckoned Pedro, one of the English-speaking waiters over to the breakfast table the morning her ship was to leave port. As he began translating her Spanish words into English, I must say, I was so amazed at what he told me that I still can hardly believe it today!

"In his broken but clear English, the young waiter informed me that 'Carmelita wants you to know that she went to a psychic reader one month ago and was told that she had to go on this particular cruise to Puerto Vallarta.

Her psychic stated that if she did, she would meet the man she would marry. She also said that his name would begin with a letter that was not in the Spanish alphabet—that would be 'W,' and that he worked around paper, lots and lots of paper. The psychic foretold her she will leave her country for him—that she would be prepared to live anywhere with him because she will love him that much. Carmelita wants you to know that learning a second language and two children were also predicted by this same psychic. Lastly, she was informed that she would live and work in a coastal city in a cold country.

"Of course I was beaming all the while this fascinating information was being translated for me. I could scarcely believe the remarkable parallel—it was very compelling. I then knew what I needed to do next. I had Pedro the waiter translate *my* story, one which was virtually a carbon-copy of Carmelita's! I started in earnest as I let the peculiar reasons behind my trip be known. It was important for me that Carmelita knew why I booked it in the first place. Through Pedro's superb translating skills, I told her that the only reason I was there was because a psychic reader in Canada persuaded me to go on a vacation to Mexico, and that I would find the woman of my dreams there—one that I would fall in love with, marry, and have two children with. By the end of the translation Carmelita was beaming even more brightly than I was! We were both ecstatic over the parallel nature of our reasons for where we were—why we were there-- and when we were there. With heavy hearts and welling eyes, we shared another indelible kiss. The waiter was genuinely dumbfounded, almost in disbelief. He told me first in English and then Carmelita in Spanish that he had never before heard such an intriguing, unbelievable love story, not even in the movies. He jokingly said "I think they should make a movie with your love story"

Chapter 12 • *Miracles Really Do Happen*

"'God works in many beautiful ways amigos. He has given you both his blessing!' the waiter told us. I tipped Pedro for his time and assistance and with a broad Mexican smile he bid us both luck for the future. Not surprisingly, we had no real appetite for the breakfast buffet before us due to the just-discovered coincidences, and anxieties, not to mention Carmelita's imminent departure. We made the most of the last few minutes together, trying to savor the shared feelings of delight and intoned promises for the future.

"After we exchanged phone numbers and addresses, several minutes of looming silence fell upon us. We said little then, preferring the quiet and serenity of the morning to speak for itself. Like young lovers, we more or less clung to one another before she finally announced it was time to make her way onboard. We walked together to the dock, along the length of it, and up to her ship's gang-plank. It was there that we held each other in tight embrace and shared yet another unforgettable kiss—a salty-sea-breeze one, as I recall. Bidding each other a fond farewell, she walked away. She stopped every few steps though to wave back at me.

"'Hasta pronto Bill!' were the last words I heard as I watched Carmelita make her way through the security check-in. Seconds later, she disappeared into the shadowed hulk of the big ship. In my heart I knew that these were tears of joy and happiness and not of sadness. It wasn't an ending; it was in fact a very beautiful and enchanting beginning, and one that changed both of our lives forever.

"Knowing that Carmelita also had written notes from her psychic reader—just the same way I had from Mary, made the whole romance seem so much more remarkable. It was not unlike a confirmation to me, in that it was all meant to be. And to think that we were both destined to the same city only because of two unrelated psychic readers two countries apart, was in itself quite a little miracle."

By now, all in the room sat astonished and everyone was eager for more. Some were on the verge of disbelief and some were mesmerized by the storybook nature of the highly unusual encounter.

Bill asked, "Am I boring anyone yet?"

All resounded with a convincing "Noooo," and, "Tell us more Bill!"

My sister remarked, "We have to hear the rest of this incredible love story—we'll probably never hear another one like it."

So we refreshed drinks and all got comfortable again and Bill went on with the rest of the story. Throughout, he exhibited no nervousness or apprehension, and in front of complete strangers too. He went about telling his tale of romance like he had the starring role in a major love story production.

"I lingered for some time there on the dock, waiting for Carmelita to set sail. As I did, I scanned the four levels of decks upon the big ship. Suddenly, she emerged from a crowd of passengers, third deck, portside. I recognized her, and her amazing smile, instantly. Until that ship had all but vanished on the horizon, we waved and transmitted kisses across the ever-widening expanse.

The rest of the day seemed to disappear, just as Carmelita did. Before I knew it, it was nightfall. I went to bed that night thinking how-on-earth we would be able to communicate over the phone with sign language! I lay in bed, in a dreamy and contented state, saying to myself—I *have* to

Chapter 12 • *Miracles Really Do Happen*

see her again and, as soon as possible. It was then I knew for a fact that I was going to Mexico City.

"I also said a prayer to myself that night to thank God for bringing us together, to ask to keep Carmelita safe, and to help us re-unite no matter what the impending difficulties may be. I already instinctively knew that watching the sunrise was never going to be the same without Carmelita by my side. I knew that for sure and I was happy to realize that watching the cruise ships dock and depart in and out of the harbour each day kept me close to her at heart. It didn't take long to cross my mind that I had to do some fast-learning of the Spanish language, particularly for the phone-calls. By daybreak, with a fresh triple-espresso in hand, I found myself asking directions to the local bookstore, hoping to acquire a pocket-sized Spanish-English dictionary. I came across a nice little souvenir shop not far from the hotel. The first thing I set my eyes upon in the tiny store was a *Travelers' Guide to Conversational Spanish*. I purchased it in a flash and headed back to my hotel.

"Needless to say, the first words I wanted to learn were, 'I love you,' 'I miss you,' and, 'How are you?' After many hours of sitting on the beach trying to concentrate on various phrases as well as my pronunciation skills I managed to learn a number of phrases with little difficulty. Believe it or not, the very next day I got up the nerve to call her and put my crash-course acquired self-schooling to the test. While I was waiting for someone to answer at the other end, I got a little jumpy and suddenly forgot how to ask for Carmelita in Spanish. When her mother answered I was completely tongue-tied. All I could think to say was, 'Carmelita? Carmelita?' I worried unnecessarily for her mother quickly called her to the phone. Meanwhile, it seemed like my heart was skipping a few beats as I was unsure if I would be able to remember all of the phrases I had practiced so persistently. I guess I must have done alright because we talked for half an hour and, surprisingly, with the same level of communication we had when we spoke in person!"

Taking a deep breath, and looking like he needed a breather, my mom brought Bill a glass of my dad's red-cherry wine. He held it up and said, "Cheers everyone." All of us raised our glasses as he added, "I would like to propose a toast to Mary—for making all my dreams come true. You are truly amazing!"

Bill's story entertained everyone and it was followed by an absolute flurry of comments and questions.

"I've got goose bumps."

"That's unbelievable! Bill, you're so lucky!"

"What a great story-line for a movie!"

"Do you think it was fate, Bill?"

It wasn't long before the words "Will You Marry Me?" were followed by a resounding 'Yes.' They were married the following summer in Mexico City. I received an invitation and was not surprised to hear that they would be having a second wedding ceremony in Canada for all of Bill's family and friends. Carmelita managed to land a job at the Canada Customs office as a translator. She adapted quickly and never had any problems fitting into Canadian culture. She learned to speak and write English exceedingly well in only her first year. And I have wonderful recollections of the many Mexican specialties she cooked for me whenever I visited them at their adobe-styled casa which over-looked the endless blue of the Pacific Ocean.

I loved reading their notes, the ones they had scribbled down from their readings. It was amazing to think how everything two readers—two countries apart—predicted for them became reality. Lending further intrigue, the readings came at almost the same time too! The psychic reader in Mexico City had told Carmelita that she would leave her country, her friends and family for the man of her dreams and he sure was right.

Bill knew how much Carmelita wanted to have children, so he almost immediately arranged for a reverse vasectomy. Carmelita finally got pregnant a few years later and had the little boy she had always dreamed of—just as her Mexican reader told her she would have. It was also the same boy I visualized Bill having with his new wife. They named him Umberto, and not too long after this child was born, Carmelita conceived again. Their second child—a little girl whom they named Carmelita after her mother!

Bill purchased a big mansion on the lower mainland of British Columbia for his lovely bride, just like the one her reader had told her she would one day live in. Bill still works at the *Vancouver Sun* Newspaper, where he plans to stay until he retires. They went on another cruise for their 25th anniversary in 2010.

And I have no doubt a place called Puerto Vallarta was on their itinerary, the place where they can relive all those beautiful and wonderful memories. "Miracles really do happen".

Chapter 13

MY BIGGEST SCEPTIC

There are times when clients have come across my path who are really and truly sceptics. Most of them still live by the old adage; "If it sounds too good to be true, then it probably is." I never try to convince this handful of people otherwise, for everyone is of course entitled to their own beliefs and I must admit I have a few myself. I can usually convince them that they are in charge of their own destiny, and can change their life's course simply by believing in themselves. Positive thinking, having an open mind, faith in God, and the powers of the universe are all parallel attributes. There are also times when a life-changing experience in a non believer's life can shatter previously held convictions. It's not uncommon for sceptics to experience unbelievable and undeniable life changing events surrounding them, soon after they have had a psychic reading. We as psychics love these transitions,, because we hear all about it word for word, detail after detail, as if they were telling us something we didn't already know..We love it. ..It makes our 'gift of intuition' even more exciting.

One such experience I'll never forget.! I was on vacation in Palm Desert for the winter, when I was introduced

Chapter 13 • *My Biggest Sceptic*

to a lovely Italian family who lived there. They were a very well known family. Gerry in the Race Car business, and Janet a Dental Hygienist. We hit it off imediatley because of our backgrounds, and so many familiarities. Her dad was Frank , my dad was Frank, Her mother's name was Millie. My mom's name was Millie. She had a daughter Julie I had a sister Julie, and this seemed to go on and on, until we became just like family in a very short time. Sitting at their Christmas dinner table became common place every winter we went to the Desert area. Consequently they later introduced me to friend of a friend. His name was Rick Johanson. He was in his late 20s at the time, nice looking, tall, dark and handsome. The perfect match for many a single woman. When he first walked in the door, I could sense that someone had put him up to it—that he really didn't want to be read. Such trepidations are typically based upon harboured fears of what I might or might not see for them.

His first words were, "You have read some of my friends for a few years now and they are always telling me that I should see you for a reading. He sat comfortably with one leg crossed and asked, "How long have you been doing this?"

"As long as I can remember," I said with a modest smile, hoping to chip away at his scepticism.

"Really?" he said with a genuine look of surprise. "If that is the case, perhaps I should just listen to—and enjoy all—you have to tell me."

"Well I'm sure you won't be sorry you came for a reading Rick. My readings are fun, exciting, adventurous and very often life-changing! Most importantly, they are something you can enjoy not just today, but for years and years to come."

Being as he was, a referral, from someone obviously happy with their reading, I had the distinct feeling that his reading was going to be all of that as well as life changing in some way.

We sat facing one another and chatted a bit about the heat of the day and how to stay cool in the Palm Springs desert. As I began to study him more intently, I started sensing vibes from his energy. I got clear messages that were mixed with visions that were equally clear, as clear as the clear blue sky. I felt mesmerized by the visions I was seeing and began blurting out everything as I was seeing it. I have no idea how long this reading lasted—it could have been close to an hour, or it may have been only twenty minutes. Such was the intensity!

"I see many changes for you, changes you are likely not going to be ready for."

Looking me straight in the eye Rick replied, "Like, what kind of changes?"

"Well I see you lying flat on your back, in terrific pain for starters. Your back is injured—possibly broken. You can't walk, and—"

It was then he cut in and said, "There is nothing wrong with my back. I'm lifting heavy things at work all day"

I was thinking to myself, *this guy doesn't want to listen to what I have to say, but I will continue anyway.* "I see you going in a helicopter. I can hear the specific sound of the rotor-blades," I said matter-of-factly.

With a perplexed look upon his face he replied, "Well... Not too likely this will be happening, I'm not crazy about flying"   "But it isn't an ordinary plane, I said trying to convince him, I see you in a "helicopter " But that's just it, I know for sure I would never, ever fly in a "helicopter". It

Chapter 13 • My Biggest Sceptic

could be my dad or someone else, but it sure won't be me!"

Wiping my brow and shaking my head, I did my best to downplay his reaction. The sound I was hearing so clearly was not of an ordinary plane. It was unmistakably that of a helicopter" and its proximity was such that it felt as though it was hovering directly above my head! The sound was clear and loud, so there was no mistaking it for anything else. At that moment, I didn't know whether to continue or quit the reading in midstream simply because he just was not enjoying it whatsoever. I decided to let him decide. "Would you rather not have this reading Rick because we can stop at any time, it is fine with me."

"Oh no, please continue. I find it amusing—it's just strange that nothing you have told me so far is anything I can relate to."

"Well that is sometimes how readings go. Then, before you know it, and when you least expect it, things begin to happen." I took a deep breath and continued on.

What I saw next I immediately knew he would not want to hear—in fact I wouldn't have blamed him if he just got up and walked right out the door. "I see a girl, a nice girl who you are in love with, but she won't be in your life long." I could see in his eyes he was crushed, not to mention the obvious disbelief. As he sat there trying hard to absorb the seemingly unlikely scenario, I advised him, "I can't sugar-coat anything. I only say what I'm feeling and what I'm seeing. Unfortunately, it's not always exactly what a person wants to hear."

By this time Rick was noticeably more anxious, waiting in a sense for the reading to be over. My heart went out to him because it was not the kind of reading he was expecting and I knew he was disappointed in what I had seen.

Taking a deep breath and a long sigh afterwards, he told me, "Well, I am indeed puzzled. We are thinking very seriously about getting married in a few months."

Turning a deaf ear and scrambling for the right words to break it to him as gently as I could, I thought to myself, *I have to just say it like I always do, only with much more empathy.* I lowered my head and took my glasses off as if to read someone their last rites. I took a deep breath and before I knew it, the words began flowing effortlessly. "You will not marry this girl. She will not be in your life. Yes, you will be very hurt." The words as I spoke them seemed to hurt me almost as much as they did him. Just seeing such a sad look on this young man's face was difficult for me.

The sad and gloomy face took on an air of determined denial. "No, I sure can't believe that part about my girlfriend"

Of course his reply wasn't at all surprising to me and I continued trying to convey what I had seen in-store for him. "You will marry one day soon and you will find your true love." I told him this with intonations of encouragement. This bright news brought an immediate shimmer of hope to his deep blue eyes. I could sense easily enough though that he was not at all happy with the reading, and I was quite sure he was wishing he had never been talked into coming in the first place. I carried on with what vibes and visions I was able to pick up on and all that came through was his house.

"I see you selling your house," I said as if I had just read it in the morning paper.   "No," he said, shaking his head. "I love my house, and I have no intentions of selling it. So...no, I can't see that either."

"I understand your scepticism Rick, but don't forget, only time will tell," I advised, as I looked at him over my

Chapter 13 • My Biggest Sceptic

glasses. "I also see you not working, staying home in fact. You are lying down, taking it easy recovering from back pain"

Straightening up in his chair, he announced, "I don't have back pain—never have. And, I'm never sitting around home simply because I'm always working. I'm lifting heavy things all day long too—I have a strong back."

By now Rick was getting restless, and I began more seriously wondering if I should end his reading before he got up and walked out the door.

"You have not told me one thing that accurately relates to me" he said as he straightened his blue jeans, and tried to get comfortable in the only comfortable chair in the apartment.

Again I said, "Only time will tell—if you want to listen to me for a moment more. I see a nurse around you Rick." I glanced at him sitting there. He was in sheer bewilderment.

Looking straight into my eyes and looking even more sad and bewildered, he said, "My girlfriend isn't a nurse"

"Well...I didn't say your girlfriend was a nurse, or even that your new girlfriend is one but, I do see a nurse around you."

At this particular point I decided to end his reading, since it was getting obvious he was only becoming more frustrated with what I had to tell him. And, as much as I found him quite easy to read, I also knew he was at that time, at that moment 'My Biggest Skeptic.'

"If you have any questions about your reading at a later date," I offered, "just give me a call, and I'll be happy to answer them for you."

He smiled as if to say, you won't be hearing from me

ever again lady, but he did bid me a polite farewell with, "Thanks, I have your number." As he made his way towards the door, he said something that I've heard many times before. "I'm sorry that I am so skeptical, but right now none of this makes any sense to me."

Taking it all with a grain of salt, I tried to reassure him. "Sometimes the readings don't make sense at the time Rick, but before too long you will see that they do indeed end up making sense!" We both chuckled at the prospect of this, and then he said goodbye and walked out to his heavy-duty work truck that was parked outside the door. I looked at the huge pickup and instantly felt there would be a different truck in the weeks to come, all of course, unbeknownst to him. I knew that everything I had seen was very real and that before long he would be frantically searching for my phone number.

It was about a week later when I was sitting poolside reading the paper when all of a sudden I had a vision of me winning a jackpot. I could see the venue as well, it was a bingo palace. We passed by the low-slung building with the oversize parking lot on the highway as we were driving into Palm Springs. When I asked my husband to drive me there, he was surprised that I had even noticed the place. He happily agreed that he could drop me off there and pick me up when it was over.

The Morongo Bingo Palace, which was 16 miles north of Palm Springs, was a huge, glitzy-looking Vegas-styled place and as soon as I entered the building I experienced a rush of adrenaline. The ensuing excitement ran through me as if I had already won the jackpot! I could see the staff working the floor. They were attired with their customary black aprons and I knew that one of them would be counting out a bundle of money from one of these aprons right

Chapter 13 • My Biggest Sceptic

into my hands. The feeling of this was so strong that when I scanned the room looking for a place to sit, I made a point of finding out where the bingo-caller was situated, so that I could position myself in close proximity. I was wanting to make sure they could hear me holler "Bingo," when I won.

Just after the first game started. I was a bit confused as to what I was supposed to be playing, but everyone close by was more than helpful in showing me the ropes. A couple hours into the game, an eary loud rumble rippled across the floor. Then the table started vibrating. A small tremor had hit and the mini-earthquake shook everything around me for what seemed minutes on end. In reality it was but a few seconds. Not having ever experienced an earthquake of any magnitude before I didn't know weather to scream, run, or hide under the table, but seeing how it stopped as fast as it came, everything and everyone went right back to normal—with the bingo-caller announcing the earthquake, and reassuring all that everything was okay. Still dazed from the fright and not feeling much like playing anymore, I happened to look up and noticed my dear husband scouting the bingo hall looking for me with what seemed an exasperated look of determination upon his face. I knew instantly something was wrong, for he never, ever came to a bingo hall looking for me. He would always be waiting in the truck outside in a designated area of the parking lot three hours later. I waved him down and got his attention. He barely had the chair beside me pulled out when he said, "You better come back to our hotel—before we get in trouble from the front-desk."

"What are you talking about?" I whispered so as not to disturb the other players sitting around me. My attempt to be discrete had virtually no effect as I could sense ears all about me which were now perking up to listen in.

"Well, the fellow you read the other night by the name of Rick— Well... he has just been in a serious motorcycle accident, and has been air-lifted by an emergency response helicopter to the trauma unit of the Palm Springs Hospital. His family, his friends, even his nurses keep calling the hotel. We are going to get kicked out of there with all those phone calls!"

"Oh No. How terrible, Is he okay, When did it happen" I said in horror like it was my own child. "So come on, lets go, get all your stuff and lets get out of here" he commanded, "Well not quite yet" I said as I continued dabbing one of my cards.

"Why not?" He scowled out loud, starting to lose his temper. "What are you waiting for?"

"Every game is for one-thousand dollars, and I see myself winning this game—that's why." Just as I was saying this to him, I noticed that one of my cards only needed a single number. I got ready. And sure enough, a few seconds later, I was hollering "Bingo" at the top of my lungs, waving my card triumphantly in the air. My heart started pounding simply from the excitement, of winning but mostly because I just heard that Rick who was my biggest skeptic was just in a horrific motorcycle accident, and all I wanted to do was go back to the hotel, phone all the people who would obviously be family and friends, to let them know Rick is going to be just fine. I would just have to convince them of that, and Rick of coarse..

As the money was being counted out to me by one of the attendants, a women sitting across the table was shaking her head, saying to her friend, "She knew she was going to win a jackpot, she said that as soon as she sat down" She must be psychic or something. Why don't we ever get premonitions like that?"

Chapter 13 • *My Biggest Sceptic*

As I went to put the money safely away in my purse, a very sweet Mexican woman—who had never said a word all night—reached across the table to rub the money so as to bring her some luck. My dear husband on the other hand, who was just minutes before getting upset that I was not ready to leave, was now shaking his head saying, "You said you were going to win a jackpot and you did. I can't believe it!"

Laughing, and trying to calm myself down, I said, "*Now* we can go dear." I picked up my belongings, said good-bye to all the well-wishers and made way for the exit with my husband and first U.S. windfall.

When we got back to our suite at the hotel, we found a note which had been taped to the door. It was only four words long. It read, "PLEASE COME TO OFFICE." My husband's first response was, "Oh great—we *are* going to get kicked out of here."

I tore the note off the door, and quietly stated, "No we're not going to be kicked out. There are probably just more messages." And with that, to the office we went.

The owners of the resort were lovely people from India. While they couldn't speak English that well, they made up for it by being exceptionally hospitable and making everyone feel welcome. When the lovely woman answered the door with her new baby in her arms, and her usual kind greeting, I happily realized she was not mad nor even the least bit upset. She handed us the list of messages under a heading that read "URGENT." Twelve names were scribbled down along with respective phone numbers. We didn't explain what it was all about, but we did apologize for the inconvenience. All she said was, "I hope this urgent time is not family sick."

"When I return these phone calls, I will know more of what has happened."

Smiling and cuddling her beautiful baby, she said, Good luck with everything."

We hurried to our suite and I started in on the calls. The list of names was of friends and relatives—and one from the hospital, where Rick was lying with his severe back injury. They all gave me the complete run down of what had happened; where, when and how. As I listened carefully, it was not unlike someone telling me about a movie I had already seen. Apparently, from that moment on, when Rick heard the sound of the helicopter hovering over his head in the darkness of the desert—flat on his back upon a stretcher—he became another one of my true believers.

The next name written was 'Station Nurse,' and when I finally got through to the right extension, I found out how he was doing. The nurse was apparently calling on Rick's behalf, just to know if I had seen a wheelchair around him. More specifically, did I see the permanence of a wheelchair? Do I see him eventually walking again? I explained it very clearly as I seen the vision of Rick back to good health, after a possible surgery, but he will be walking his back will recover and be as strong as it ever was" This was my repeated explanation all day long and for many days after.. I answered all these questions, and more, knowing that once they were relayed back to Rick they would provide a calming and healing effect for him. The station nurse was elated upon hearing that I did see a successful recovery with no wheelchair and my confirmation that, "Yes, he will walk."

Luckily, I was staying in the desert for another month and I was happy to be able to reassure and support Rick if he needed it. I was also an information hub for him during his recovery in hospital. His relatives and many friends were still phoning me weeks later to ask questions regard-

Chapter 13 • My Biggest Sceptic

ing his recovery and progress. It was sad to think that such a big, strong, and physically fit young man could be flat on his back for several weeks in possible need of more than one surgery. But at the same time I knew it could have been much worse, had it not been for his guardian angels who were riding with him on that motorcycle in the desert that night. His best friend who was riding along with him, was definitely one of his guardian angels, because without him sprinting up to the highway to flag down help, who knows how long he would have been stranded in the middle of the dark desert, unable to walk. Funny as it may sound, his friend John who happened to be riding his bike right behind him that night, was the one who gave Rick my name and number. The first time I read John, which was years earlier, I told him, "One day you will save someone's life." After hearing this story, I felt sure this was the life he saved.

Several weeks passed and his recovery was coming along just great when another event from his reading began to unfold; only this time it wasn't involving broken bones, but rather a broken heart. His fiancée had suddenly left him and even though I had told him of this fate, it was still quite a blow when it actually happened.

John said he talked about this incident for many years. In particular, about how he had been so sceptical at the time of the reading only to later realize that everything had happened to him just the way I had seen it. Many years have since passed and, I have unfortunately lost touch of Rick. The last time I did hear was in the early 90's I heard he had made a complete recovery. He has a thriving business, a beautiful loving wife, and a couple of lovely children. By all accounts, he is extremely happy. And, by all accounts, they were quite sure he is a believer in destiny, the universe and, intuition.

Chapter 14

NEVER SAY NEVER

One day while on a winter vacation in San Deigo California, I noticed an elderly gentlemen sitting quietly by himself at the resort swimming pool. Being the out-going person that I am, I smiled and said, "Hi there," and made some small talk about the weather and where we were from. He introduced himself as Tony and before I knew it, we were talking away about everything from politics to relationships. It was as though we had met in another lifetime since both of us felt as if we had been friends for years. For some reason, I felt that this man was going to have a story; a story that not only he would tell me about, but one that he would allow me to write about in my diary. And that he did. By the next day, while my husband was out golfing, this friendly and out going man and I found ourselves sitting out poolside sipping a cold drink, reading the gossip papers, and exchanging small talk, and it wasn't long before he began to tell me his life-story which had me almost in tears on more than one occasion.

"I was married thirty-five years. We had three beautiful daughters. I am proud to say we had a happy life. I was never unfaithful to my wife, but I have always thought about a woman who I fell in love with forty-some years

Chapter 14 • Never Say Never

ago. I have always felt deep in my heart that someday our paths would meet again and we would be together. I'm still convinced that we both fell in love the minute we were introduced. But, she was a married woman—to a man I worked with in fact. I was still single at the time. I sensed the energy, the sheer chemistry of the contact, the minute we shook hands. I never tried to look her up since either. It's just not my style, interfering with another man's wife. I married shortly after that and I've never seen her, or heard from her, since that day. I have to admit there were several times throughout my marriage in which I wondered if she ever thought about me—even remembered me for that matter. I always wondered if she was happy. Was she still married or, even still alive for that matter."

Tony paused, obviously reflecting upon his own spoken words. I seized the vacant moment to ask him a straight-up question.

"Do you believe in fate or destiny Tony?"

"Oh yes, indeed. I have heard many stories of how people find one another just by chance. How certain people simply seem destined to be together."

"All you have to do is think in a positive light. Visualize her standing beside you, holding your hand and talking to you. Leave the rest up to the universe and if it is meant to be, it will be"

Just sitting there listening to his sad but beautiful story. I could sense a connection to the woman he was obviously still in love with. For some reason words were flying out of my mouth that came out of nowhere. He was getting all choked up, as he tried to tell me more about their first and last meeting so many years before. Searching through the sun lotions and snack foods in my bag, I found him some tissues.

"I feel a bit embarrassed telling you all this—you're probably somewhat bored by it already." He said as he wiped away the tears in his watery blue eyes.

Shaking my head in disagreement, I laughed and replied, "Actually, I think I was meant to meet you Tony."

Before I could say another word, he went on to say, "I've been doing a lot of praying since I lost my wife and…I have actually broke down and told my daughters about this woman." He said as he cleared his throat. "They told me that their mother would be so happy to know I was happy again. They let me know that they are all behind me. And unequivocally so too! They said they would be happy for me if I could spend the rest of my life with someone I love."

"How thoughtful and kind of your daughters Tony" accepting someone new in your life." "They are truly wanting you to be happy for the rest of your life, and I think that is wonderfull"

"Well they know that no one will ever replace their mother, and I don't expect them, nor want them, to ever think otherwise. But, I know I'm very lucky to have such altruistic daughters. They genuinely care about me. You know, I have had two near-death experiences. In both of these close calls, I saw the oft-cited white light—and a tunnel too. In this tunnel there was a woman. I somehow learned her name—it was Marie. She was wearing a flowing white gown. She was approaching, coming towards me. In an instant, Marie was in right in front of me, not more than ten-feet away. She reached forward offering her hand, calling out—'Hang-on Tony, hang-on…'"

By this time, more tears were welling up, and he was having trouble just getting the words out of his mouth. I knew at this very minute however that he *was* going to have this woman in his life. I had a clear vision of her sit-

Chapter 14 • Never Say Never

ting beside him, holding his hand. I also knew that I was going to be recording this story in my diary. I wanted to make sure I had it accurate, word for word as they say.

Tony continued on, but now with more analysis. "I feel certain that the only reason I never died, was because of the incredible energy of her touch. It felt like heat from the sun, penetrating through every cell in my body."

Clearing my voice and fighting back some tears myself, I said, "I know the feeling Tony. I have been there myself."

"Really!" he said with genuine interest. "I knew there was a reason we met. Maybe it's just so that we can talk about our near-death experiences. If that isn't it, I'm sure there is a reason yet that we managed to meet each other."

"There is almost always a reason different people come into your life." I said as I got up from my chair.

"Where are you going? he asked, looking concerned, "I hope I'm not scaring you away!"

"Oh no, not at all actually. Have no fear Tony, I'm only in search of my writing journal. I need to make some notes!"

"That's great, because I want to finish telling you my story of how I almost died. No one else it seems can relate to it unless they have actually been there themselves."

By now I had many questions for this poor man who was still so desperately in love after thirty-five years and, who was pouring his heart out to me—a perfect stranger. Furthermore, he had yet to learn that I was a psychic reader. So I listened very carefully to the details that he seemed to be remembering so clearly. He talked about it as though it was the day before. His memories were fresh and vivid, making it easy for me to visualize his story.

"I was only in my early twenties. I was working in a mine on the west coast—Vancouver BC, in fact. A friend from the mine introduced me to this beautiful lady. One evening, we all sat around a big table enjoying a couple of drinks. It was a quaint little bar, very romantic with nice soft music playing. After talking to this attractive woman for only a few minutes, I became aware that something magical had happened to both of us. I had never before experienced such chemistry in my life. There was a palpable energy about us—between us to be specific. And you know, I have always felt that it was something more than merely my imagination.

"Years went by and I didn't want to waste all my life away clinging to the hope of one day seeing this woman again. So, I did eventually get married, to a wonderful woman but, never did I again experience that same kind of magical energy I had that unforgettable day—that day I was introduced to Marie. Since my wife died, I seem to be thinking about her all the time, and I'm now living with the hope that one day my prayers will be answered. I know it must sound ridiculous, and I have even been thinking of seeing a counsellor over this—just in case I am in some kind of depression over the loss of my wife. Sometimes I feel a bit guilty, for thinking about her so often, instead of my wife that is. I know it all sounds strange, and excuse me for pouring all this onto you—especially considering that I just met you—but it seems that I only have a one-track mind these days. I'm sorry. "

"Don't be sorry," I said, "just be thankful that you have those beautiful and unforgettable memories, that you've had tucked away in your heart for so many years. Many people in their whole lifetime will never get to experience such a feeling".

As I sat there looking at him getting more burnt by the minute, I wondered if this was the right time to tell him that I was giving him a reading without him knowing it. I was picking up vibes and I was seeing all kinds of visions for him. I didn't hesitate in telling him what I had just seen. "You might not believe this Tony, but you are going to see her again. In fact, you will not only see her again, you will spend the rest of your life with her!"

By now tears were streaming down the lines of his face, and he looked me straight in the eye and said, "You say that as though you really mean it."

"Yes I most certainly do Tony." It was at that moment that I felt the need to tell him I was a psychic reader.

"Oh my goodness, I can't believe I'm actually talking to a real psychic."

"Well, now you can say you have met and talked to one."

I continued to see visions of this little lady and described her in detail; however I couldn't seem to pick up her whereabouts. Not yet anyway. By the end of the day, I had him pretty much convinced that his guilt was normal. I also encouraged him to remember that his wife is now dead, and he and Marie are very much alive.

"I see you and Marie sitting in my living room."

"In *your* living room?" Tony exclaimed. "You mean, up in Canada?"

"That's what I said, "In my living room, up in Canada."

"I have always known through a mutual friend where she was living, but I've recently lost contact with that person—don't even know if she is still alive."

At that point I asked him, "Would you be interested in putting all these thoughts of her down on paper? You could write it in the form of a love letter."

Looking at me as if he'd just seen a ghost, he asked, "Why?"

"Well, I see you writing her a beautiful letter. And, I can see her reading it."

Tony hesitated, then spoke with rising enthusiasm, "Well...that would be a nice thing to do...yes...yes, why not? I can do that tonight. I have not great handwriting though; any chance you could transcribe it for me?"

"No, there is no need to do that Tony, and besides, I can guarantee you she will like it much better in *your* handwriting."

"Boy-oh-boy, you really do see this don't you?"

"You bet I do," I said, as I jotted down a few more notes.

The sun was going down fast and furious and a cruising wind started to swirl dust around the pool deck so we decided to call it an afternoon and agreed to see each other again the following day. Bidding me good afternoon and thanking me for listening, Tony smiled broadly with newfound optimism.

"I want to go get started—writing down my thoughts about Marie. Tomorrow I will show them to you."

The next morning arrived with another stunning sunrise. I peered out the window and there was Tony sitting out at the patio, under the palm tree that was like a post card. Coffee cup in one hand, and writing pad in the other. As I took a deep breath of fresh clean air, and could sense that something magical was going to happen with Tony, and I was actually getting excited for him. I hadn't told him yet that I was leaving the next day for Palm Springs. On my way out the door I jotted down my phone number and address on a little piece of paper, knowing he was going to need it when he came to visit me in Vernon.

"Good morning Mary; "How are you today"? He asked with a beaming glow in his eyes. "I'm just fine thanks,

Chapter 14 • *Never Say Never*

and will be even finer when I read what you have in your hands" I said jokingly as I sat on the chair he pulled out for me. "Well, I wrote down my thoughts of Marie last night, just as you said, It made me feel as though she was right beside me. It actually sounds pretty good. Can I read it to you?"

"If you would like to share it with me, that's great Tony, but don't feel obligated."

Looking at me with the saddest eyes ever he replied, "Well I would really like to know what you think." With misty eyes he opened up his folded white piece of paper, and read me the most beautiful love letter I'd ever heard. I was getting misty-eyed myself as I sat there listening. He finished reading the eloquent words he had scribed and folded the paper back up saying, "Do you really think I will be able to locate her again after all these years?"

"Yes you will, but you will have to locate your friend first, as it is he who knows where Marie lives."

"Oh thank you so much for giving me such hope. I'll get in touch with my friend Tom the day I get home," he announced, as he took a sip of his coffee.

"Tony, you have to promise me one thing."

He then looked directly at me, appearing a bit perplexed. "What is that"?

"You have to think positive and start visualizing. Visualize the two of you holding hands in a private and cozy atmosphere."

"That will be easy dear, because I visualize those kinds of thoughts all the time anyways!"

"I'm sure you do Tony, but you have to combine the visualizing with the positive thinking. Thinking that you are going to find her and visualizing the two of you together. 'I wish,' or 'I might,' or 'maybe,' must never enter the equation. Instead, it's all about 'I will,' and 'I am going to.'

"When do you think we will be together?"

"Well," I said, taking another deep breath, "the universe has its own time schedule. We can't as human beings control that but," I said laughing, "it will be when it is *meant* to be, and not a moment before. Once you find the address for her, you can mail this beautiful letter directly to her. Afterwards, I see you getting your life back."

"Are you sure that my letter wont aggravate her life. I mean, you know, cause any problems for her. What if she's married!" and happy where she is?"

"No, I don't see that. I see her absolutely ecstatic about receiving a letter from you."

After reassuring him once again, fortifying the belief that his life will dramatically change once he mails the letter, he said, "Yes, you are right. I can't wait to go home now, so I can look up some people who may have her current address. You know, believe it or not, I've been thinking about doing this ever since my wife died, but never had the nerves to go through with it. But now that I have actually put all my thoughts about her down in writing, I'm actually excited about putting a stamp on it and getting it into the mail box. I'm beginning to realize that I must have met you for this very reason."

I laughed again, and said, "I'm happy to have met you too Tony, because it proves to me yet again, that there is always 'hope if there is love', and true love never dies"

As we continued talking, I had another vision, and one that was as clear as a bell. It was a remarkable vision, one of Marie actually sitting with me in my sunroom, back home in Canada; a cup of tea in her right hand, and the letter from Tony in the other. My vision of her was that of

Chapter 14 • Never Say Never

a caring and gentile, and fragile looking woman, possibly in her late sixties. Her voice was coming through strong and clear. And, she was smiling and so very happy. I was totally convinced by this point and, so excited for the two of them, because I knew for sure they would be together.

Tony was overwhelmed upon hearing what I had just seen that he was literally crying tears of joy. He kissed the letter he had written, gave me a big hug, and said, "Thank-you, thank-you, thank-you."

At that very moment I savoured Tony's obvious joy. Seeing the sparkle of happiness in his eyes was truly rewarding. He appeared as if someone had just breathed life into him—a new life. It also confirmed for me that I was doing exactly what I was meant to be doing; using and sharing my gift to help others all over the world. In any possible way, be it big or small. It's not only about *creating* happiness; it's also about *reviving* it. Usually the happiness is there, it's just obscured and, if left that way, at risk of loss. Having the ability to give someone back the happiness they have lost somewhere along the line, is a colossal satisfaction for me. There is no greater reward than this.

Our time in San Diego ended sooner than I would have liked, but I was happy to have had this special time with such an interesting man— I subconsciously knew my mission was over at that point anyway. I also realized it was no accident that we met as there are hundreds of other resorts that we could have stayed at. The morning that I left we had one last cup of coffee together out by the pool. We confirmed we had each others phone numbers and addresses as we hugged and said our goodbyes. It almost seemed as though we had been friends our whole life.

"We only have one life, and we must live it to the fullest every day; Right"? Tony asked as he gave me a hug.

"Absolutely" and always listen to your little voice inside, because it is always right"

"I don't need to tell you to stay in touch, because I know you will." I said as my husband motioned me that the car was all packed up and ready to go. I turned, and slowly walked away down the pool deck, feeling a bit melancholy to be leaving, but happy for Tony and his future. I knew in my heart, that I would be seeing him with Marie by his side the next time I seen him.

It wasn't even a month later when Tony called to tell me that he had in his hand a letter from Marie! They were going to be getting together later that week, as she lived some 400 miles away from him. He was ecstatic, jubilant, and could hardly speak at times from fighting back tears of happiness.

"I want you to meet her Mary." I have told her all about you, and how you convinced me to find her after all these years"

I sat there at my phone-desk awash in happiness for the both of them. All I could say was, "I'd love to meet her Tony."

That day was one I will never forget. I smiled with satisfaction at the sight of the two of them as they walked in my door. Their aura was one of radiated love. Of the kind you only see in the classic movies with the likes of Clark Gable and Elizabeth Taylor. They immediately gave me a big hug. Marie was exactly like in my vision. I made tea for them as we sat in the living room, talking about the incredible odds of them finding each other after thirty five years. We must have sat for three hours or more, analyzing and talking about their lives and how they were always thinking about one another. What amazed me the most was how after all that time, they had only the memory of a hand shake and

Chapter 14 • *Never Say Never*

the subsequent energy it had generated. It was remarkable indeed to see this very same energy between the two of them so many years later.

Marie was the sweetest little lady with the softest voice, and she made it quite clear to Tony that he had been on her mind many times throughout her life as well.

"You don't know how many times throughout my troubled life I imagined this day, but to be honest, I thought it would never happen, not in a million years. Then, I got divorced—just last year. Since then, I've wondered if there might be a chance, however slim, that we would connect again. But, I didn't have the foggiest idea of where to begin looking for Tony. I've always believed in miracles, and prayed that someday I would run into this man that captured my heart when I was just a young girl. I imagined many times that someday I would be with Tony."

She was definitely everything and more than he had said about her. They made the sweetest couple, and to see such genuine affection between them made me think of a new slogan: "True love never dies, it just goes on hold."

Everyone deserves a love like this, no matter what age or against what odds. You just have to have Faith, Hope, and Love. Of course, patience, prayer, and a positive attitude help along the way. We need to believe in the dynamic powers of the universe, and our inner voice, our premonition, and intuition. It works every time and, like my dear ole dad used to say, "Never Say Never."

Chapter 15

LOVE-STRUCK IN THE DESERT

"Why can't I just find a nice guy? I never seem to have any luck when it comes to men." These all too familiar words seemed to echo coldly throughout the house this warm summer day as Dora pranced down the hallway following me to my reading room.

"I don't think I will ever find a man to love and cherish. I always seem to find the wrong man," she exclaimed even louder than before as if I were deaf. By the time we got to my bright and cheery lavender reading room however, where rose-scented candles floated in a water fountain basin and soft music played in the background, her tone of voice and whole demeanour seemed to change. She became quieter. She became calmer. By all appearances one could almost say she was in a trance. Perhaps it was the serenading sound of the background flute music. Or, it could have been the tranquil sounds of the flowing water which trickled down beside the palm tree towering behind her seat. It was a lush and relaxing ambiance and perhaps it was the combination of all these things together. Of course, I intentionally create my reading rooms to be this way and, believe me; the therapeutic benefits of such a surrounding are not restricted to only my clients!

Chapter Number • Love-Struck in the Desert

As I was preparing the tarot cards, and getting ready to read this very interesting woman, I asked her the first question without any hesitation. "Dora, why are you so hard on yourself?"

Looking at me somewhat confused as to why I had asked such a question, yet eager to answer, she replied, "Well, you see, it's like this, I am kind of interested in someone. Problem is, he doesn't seem to be very interested in me. He's a neighbour, and I really like him a lot. And...well....I don't know if we will ever be together. We have had dinners together, if I make them, and he does cut my lawn. He never seems to want anything for it either."

Before Dora could say another word, I jumped in with, "Dora, could you please show me a picture of him, before we go any further." I seemed to just know that she was wasting her time, because I could see visions of her living a lavish lifestyle and living in the States, nothing like the life she was living. Not even faintly.

"Oh yes, for sure," she squealed as she began searching into her big over sized purse for her wallet.

"Are you sure you want to see it now?" she asked hesitantly, as she held it upside down in her hand. "I wasn't going to show you until the reading was over."

"Believe me, it won't make any difference whatsoever to your reading." I realized that the reason she didn't want to show me the photo was because she was worried it might affect what I say.

I didn't look at the picture for longer than 3 seconds, before saying, "This is not the man you will be spending the rest of your life with Dora."

"Oh, No. Don't tell me this...are you sure?" she asked, her voice rising.

"Yes I'm sure. This man is only a neighbor, and just a friend, and always will be just a friend"

"Just a friend!" she echoed in a loud drawn-out tone. "What do you mean by that?"

"I mean that you will be moving away, and he will no longer be your neighbour. Not exactly the words you wanted to hear, but you did ask," I added, as I handed her back the photograph.

As the reading went on, I couldn't help but notice how sweet she really was. Her 'Barbie' curves and clothes made her look more like a hip and happening socialite of about mid 40 rather than someone the age of 62. Her eyes were a captivating emerald-green which were more than capable of swooning any man off his feet. It wasn't long before I got a vision that even I was excited about. A tall, slim built tanned faced white-haired gentleman standing beside her, came into my vision. He was wearing dark green golf slacks, white shoes, and a yellow shirt. I began to describe to Dora my interesting vision just as though I was watching it on television.

"He is a widower who loves golf. And, he typically plays where famous people frequent." As fast as the words were coming out of my mouth, Dora was scribbling them down while asking me to slow down so she could get it all straight. Momentarily oblivious to Dora being with me in the room, I went on describing this gentleman and, while doing so, felt as if I already knew him.

"You will never, ever have to worry about money," I explained, "because he has an endless supply of it from a well established business. You will be very wealthy, happy, and live somewhere in the United States. I see the both of you in a warm climate, so it's definitely the southern US."

Chapter Number • Love-Struck in the Desert

She interrupted the trance I seemed to be in, by saying, "I hate to tell you this dear, but there is nobody in Sicamous that fits that description!"

"I don't doubt it." I said, laughing. "This man you will meet is from the States."

"Well how-on-earth will I meet him if he lives in the States—I have no money to travel anywhere right now."

"He will be in Canada when you meet him," I said with a smile. She looked up at me every few seconds from her notes while doing her best to scribble down my every word.

"Dora, I see you getting an eye-drop treatment from an ophthalmologist," I announced.

Before I could say another word Dora yelled out excitedly, "I know what that is! Funny you say this since I have been thinking of getting my eyes checked for a while now, and just recently too! What else do you see in-store for me?"

Clearing my voice, I started in. "A doctor has something to do with the man you will meet."

"Oh my goodness. Are you telling me that I'm actually going to meet a doctor?"

"No. This man I am picking up—the one standing beside you—is *not* a doctor. You will be introduced to him very soon by way of a perfect stranger. This gentleman travels all over the world from what I can see. He is a widower and he is alone."

I continued receiving visions layered with little messages. And, they were loud and clear in my head—as vivid and clear as if he was standing in the room with us.

"I see him buying you a diamond ring. He will spoil you beyond words, and I see you feeling not unlike a queen as a consequence!"

The scenario I could see was detailed enough and my descriptions of it kept streaming. By this time Dora was beside herself with excitement. Tears of happiness could be seen in her eyes.

"He will want to buy you everything you see." I went on.

"Oh really?" she exclaimed, wiping her eyes and finding her voice. "I've never, ever been spoiled so that would sure be a wonderful change for me." Looking me straight in the eye, she said, "Can I ask you just one more question?"

"Of course you can Dora, but I already know what your question is."

"You do?" she laughed.

"Yes," I said with a chuckle, "you want to know if you have to move to the States in order to meet this man, and the answer is very clearly no, absolutely not. About your next vacation; you will be doing something different. Not the usual all-inclusive, far away-place thing either. It will be somewhere where there is the ocean nearby, and where there are tall stately buildings and a big bustling city. The man you are going to meet will be there. He will fall in love with you the minute he sees you!"

Once again I had him in view. He was wearing those colorful-green slacks that looked like classic golf attire. White leather golf-shoes confirmed it.

"I see an image of a logo of some kind on the pocket of his shirt. It looks like a *Polo* shirt, and its pale yellow. He must be a golfer! I can see that he is an older gentleman who has aged very well. He has a different name; it starts with a 'B.' He works around, or with, computers. He has a very kind facial expression and sparkling green eyes. I'm thinking he must live where there is sunshine year-round since I see him sporting a deep bronze tan."

Dora laughed and said, "It looks like one of my sons is going to have a camper for a couple of months, because after hearing all this I want to be sure to find this man." Still writing away, adding to her notes, she continued with, "All three of my sons live in beautiful high-rises right near the oceanfront in the heart of Vancouver."

"Fantastic!" I said with a grin. "You won't need to spend money on accommodations. I'm happy to hear that you're already thinking positive Dora."

"I feel as though I actually have something to look forward to now," she said with a smile that could win-over anyone. Pulling from her purse a compact mirror, she meticulously touched up her lipstick. "I'm so excited now. In fact, I think while I'm in Vancouver I'm going to make an appointment with an ophthalmologist. I've been thinking very seriously for some time now about investing in some contact lenses, because I'm ready to get rid of these glasses"

"Great idea!" I said, as I watched her happily primp in the mirror.

As usual—when I have such clear and exciting visions—I got carried away and in one of my trance-like modes, I lost track of time. I suggested we end the session and call it a day. Even at that, she still had a dozen or more questions along the lines of, "How old is this man? Does he have children? Where will I live?"

I answered as though I'd already met the man myself. "He is about ten years older than you Dora, but don't say that he is too old for you. When you meet him, you'll quickly realize his age will have nothing to do with your feelings for him. The answer to your second question is, I see him with only one child, a son who adores his father. But you won't have to worry about winning him over, because he will be absolutely ecstatic to see his dad find a partner."

"Thank God for that because I would sure hate to come between a father and son who have a strong bond. I'm so excited over all of this! I suppose the reason I can't quite completely believe all of this, is because my entire life has been somewhat of a struggle, so if all this happens the way you say it will, then it will be like a dream come true, and my prayers will be answered"

A few months later I was at the grocery store when all of a sudden Dora came to mind. In fact, over the course of the day her name and image came to me several times. When my phone rang that evening I knew instinctively it was her on the other end of the line. I somehow knew she was going to tell me a very exciting love story. I picked up the receiver saying, "Hi Dora!"

The voice on the other end was indeed her. "You knew it was me? Oh my gosh, how did you ever remember me so quickly? Do you remember that I live in Sicamous?"

Ignoring the second question, I replied with anticipation. "Yes, of course I remember you. How are you doing?"

"You won't believe what happened to me, while spending time with my boys in Vancouver."

"Well, I probably will. Go ahead, I'm listening," I said, as I poured myself another cup of tea, knowing this could take awhile.

"Well, I shopped until I dropped everyday. I visited with some old friends, went over to the North Shore on the sky-train. What a marvellous experience it all was. I dined-in mostly and made myself useful preparing meals for one of my sons—something I hadn't done for him since he

Chapter Number • Love-Struck in the Desert

moved out on his own. I simply just enjoyed myself; relaxing, swimming in the pool and the ocean, but nothing else happened that first week. So, I found an ophthalmologist and made my appointment. Right from the time I arrived in Vancouver, I kept thinking how nice it would be not to wear thick glasses anymore. Later that week, I had a phone call from my daughter who wanted me to spend a week with her and the grand children. I packed up and spent another wonderful week seeing the sights, going to the theatre, and walking the sea wall. I was enjoying myself, but again I didn't experience anything unusual or eventful that week either. To be completely honest, I was beginning to think your forecast for me was incorrect, and that I had wasted my time, money, and energy going on a trip to Vancouver on such a whim. Anyway I thought it only right that you should be the first to know what happened on my *third* week. Are you sitting down.?"

"Yes I'm sitting down," I replied, listening to her happy laughter, "but why don't you come over, so we can talk in person."

"You have time? Oh, that would be great! I'm just making my way through Vernon, on my way home from Vancouver, so that would be perfect. I will see you in fifteen to twenty minutes I would guess."

Hanging up the phone, I went to get my tape-recorder. I wanted to archive the details of what was undoubtedly going to be a very interesting story. Whenever I felt there was a love story that was remarkable, or miraculous, I always recorded it straight from the person telling it. Subconsciously, I knew that someday I would write a book on extraordinary love stories, and I had the feeling that this story of Dora's would surely be in it.

We greeted each other at the door with a hug and I invited her in. When I asked, "Do you mind if I record your story?" she gave me a big smile.

"I'm flattered it means that much to you."

The moment we had made our way into my reading room, I put my little cassette recorder on record. I had already staged a lit, floating aromatic candle and some fresh cut Tiger Lilies from my garden in the middle of the table. We both got comfortable in my over-stuffed arm chairs, and she wasted no time starting in on her amazing love story.

"I almost called you a couple of times," she said, laughing out loud, "but I didn't want to bother you. Anyways, it pretty much all took place on the third week of my little vacation break to Vancouver. I was beginning to panic you know, simply because my days were running out and I still hadn't had anything out of the ordinary happen. My appointment with the eye-doctor was my last thing to do before heading back home, so I worked in everything else before it, so that it would be the last stop of the day. I had to take three buses to get from Seymour Street to the doctor's office. When I finally got off the bus, I was so fascinated with the high-rises and sky-scrapers, that I walked right past where I needed to go. Anyway, after finding the right office on the 13th floor, I noticed that no one else was in the waiting room and, no one was behind the reception counter. I was quite happy with the realization that I would likely not be waiting long for my appointment, or so I thought. In fact, I ended up sitting there for almost half-an-hour. Finally, the door opened and a man came in. He was about sixty-five, years of age, tall, tanned, and very handsome looking. Being polite, I said hello and he kindly nodded right away with a hello back to me. It was then that I noticed that he was wearing green slacks with a cream collared polo shirt. As soon as I realized this, my heart skipped a couple beats since I clearly remembered your description of the golf attire. Somewhat stunned, I recovered quickly. I was captivated with this guy yet I wondered where it might possibly lead. Moments later, he sat down and I frantically fished for something to start a conversation with. And the funny words that seemed to just pop out of my mouth were, 'I hope your appointment is after mine, because I have been waiting for half-an-hour already.' He laughed out loud and told me, 'Oh, I don't have an appointment, I'm a friend. As a matter of fact I just flew in from Palm Springs, and I'm only here to go for dinner with the good doctor"

'Oh really? Well now you're talking my language because I'm starving.'

"I couldn't believe these words came out of my mouth, as I'm not usually that forward! Before I could say another word, the doctor came from out of the other room and greeted his friend with a big friendly handshake asking him, 'Do you two know each other?'

'No, we just met,' we both said, almost in unison. Before the doctor could say another thing, this nice looking white haired gentleman introduced himself to me as Bill, and the Doctor held his hand out to me and said, 'And I'm Doctor Chambers. And you must be "Mrs Cloud"

I corrected him immediately saying, I'm pleased to meet you as well Dr. but, it's Miss McCloud. Just as I was about to go into the room with the doctor, a small miracle happened. Would you believe Bill, this handsome looking man who was taking his friend Dr Chambers out for dinner, asked if I' would like to join them for dinner, can you even imagine that? I was so shocked, I didn't know how to answer. I remember looking at the doctor and asking,

'Are you okay with me coming along?' When he answered with a convincing, 'Sure, why not,' I thought I was dreaming, because let's face it, how often do you hear of such spontaneous dinner invitations!"from a Dr and a patient, and a perfect stranger going to dinner together" I mean come on lets face it , when the Dr called me Mrs. Cloud, maybe he meant to say, Mrs. Cloud 9"

Trying to control myself was getting harder by the minute. I could see the emotional delight in Dora's eyes by now, and I could tell she had even more story to tell. "I can imagine how ecstatic you must have been; suddenly realizing you were going out for dinner with two perfect strangers!" One of which you were captivated with"

"You're absolutely right , I was shocked—happily shocked that is!" she replied, catching her breath from the excitement of the story.

"We had a beautiful evening. It was a lovely dinner at a quaint little Italian Restaurant overlooking the ocean. I'm leaving a lot out as you can imagine, but the rest is history. Bill and I have just spent the last three weeks together in Vancouver and, we are very much in love! He has asked me to marry him and I have accepted, but I still can't get over how everything happened so fast, and, how Bill ended up being precisely as he was in your vision! You said this man would have money, and you were right again—he has been very successful in the computer business for many years. You said I would be spoiled, and spoiled I am already, In fact, I quickly learned to watch what I say when we walk past jewelry stores or the likes, because he wants to buy *everything* for me. He is the love of my life, and I can't believe how things have changed because of my reading. It's been dramatic actually. And, I owe it all to you Mary, and the amazingly accurate visions you saw for me."I just

Chapter Number • *Love-Struck in the Desert*

can't believe that I have met the man I will spend the rest of my life with, I keep having to pinch myself to make sure I'm not dreaming"

Of course, there is nothing more satisfying than hearing such stories, especially when I was in the center of it all, it really makes me even wonder where they would be if they hadn't been read.

A few weeks later Dora phoned again to say she was in the area and asked if she could stop by for another visit. I was delighted of course, looking forward to seeing her again and hearing more details of her beautiful love story. When I met her at the door, I couldn't believe my eyes. Dora looked fabulous, ten years younger in fact. She was lightly tanned, her hair was cut short and styled differently and, she was no longer wearing glasses. You could certainly tell she was madly in love.

"The details were uncanny, all the little things that were exactly like your vision, I mean. Remember when you told me that he would be wearing white shoes? Well, guess what? He *was* wearing white shoes."

Smiling as I was listening, I felt genuinely excited for her and, happy for myself as well, knowing that I hadn't lost my touch, a worry that had troubled me after my bout with cancer, surgery and anaesthetic.

Dora continued with her amazing story, looking straight into my eyes like she didn't want me to miss a word. She went on telling me what I had envisioned.

"You said he would be a widower; well, his wife died six years ago. You said he would be a bit older; he is sixty-nine. You also said that he would have a son. Not only is this true, but this son of his is happy for his dad and, wants to meet me. And are you ready for the really unbelievable part? He wants to build me a dream home in Palm Springs! You seemed convinced that I would be moving away and that someday I would be living in my dream house, well, I am in the midst of going home to put my house up for sale, and begin packing."

"Wow," I said, "this truly is an amazing story. It's just like a movie. I'm so happy for you Dora, and if I ever get my book written I'm sure you will be in it."

"I would love to be in your book," she exclaimed, giving me a hug. "Do you want to see what he gave me last week?"

"Sure," I answered, patiently waiting for her to open the drawstring of the little red velvet pouch she retrieved from her purse. She tipped the pouch into the palm of her hand and out tumbled a loose jumble of stunning diamonds.

"He gave me all of these diamonds out of a ring he once wore so that I could have a custom ring made for me."

"Well all I can say is, you are a very lucky woman, and he is a lucky man.

I'm very happy for the both of you."

With eyes glistening, she stated, "I can't thank you enough for insisting I make that trip to visit my boys, if I hadn't gone none of this would have happened"

We said our goodbyes, and exchanged addresses. This was the last time I saw the future bride-to-be, but a few months after the visit, I received a beautiful postcard from Dora, saying that they were in the midst of building the dream house on the outskirts of Palm Springs. They made it very clear that next time I found myself visiting the 'city in the desert' to be sure to look them up.

She signed it; *Love Struck in the Desert, Dora & Bill.*

Chapter 16

THE GREATEST GIFT OF ALL

How do you tell your best friend that you don't want her to marry the man she is engaged to, loves, and is about to get married to, only a few weeks later? How do you explain to her how necessary such advice is? How does one convince such a friend that she needs to call the wedding off, simply because you're positively sure she is marrying the wrong man? You see her with someone else, but of course *her view* is a galaxy away! I wasn't sure if I could do it, but I had to try. I had to get my nerve up before it was too late. I didn't want her to make the biggest mistake of her life so, what else was I to do?

It all happened one day when I was walking up the street in my home town of North Vancouver, British Columbia, to meet a friend for coffee. I happened to notice a beautiful royal blue 1958 Chevy Impala driving past and never thought much about it, other than admiring the lines and color of the car. After the coffee rendezvous with my friend, walking back down the street, I noticed that it was parked in front of the local pool hall. I stopped to have a better look at the old classic and noticed a man still sitting inside. Upon seeing me he got out, smiled, and started talking to me about his car. I noticed he was not only very charming, but also very confident. On top of that, he had a magnetic personality and big captivating emerald-green eyes. I asked him his name, and when he replied, "I'm Jack" I instantly had a vision of him with my friend, Helen—the same best friend who was engaged and unwittingly about to make the biggest mistake of her life. From the moment I met her fiancé I simply did not see him as part of her picture. Subconsciously, I knew that if I could just get Helen to meet this man standing in front of me, she would be captivated by him, sufficiently so that the man she was engaged to would be instant history.

I chatted a few minutes longer with my new acquaintance Jack, anxious to start asking some personal questions. The first one that popped out of my mouth was,

"Don't mind me asking Jack, but are you single?"

The smile on his face turned to a look of surprise and he quickly answered, "No, I'm a happy bachelor, and I want to stay that way."

Under my breath I said to myself, "Not for long Mr. Jack"

Fumbling for words and not wanting to embarrass him any further than I already had, I took a deep breath and heard the words in my head saying, "What have you got to lose. Ask him, it's now, or never."

So I blurted the words out of my mouth before I had time to think about them. I really wouldn't have blamed him if he told me to go fly a kite. "Jack, I know someone who you would just love to meet."

"How do you know I want to meet someone?" he said, laughing as he walked around his car.

"Well, because I just know you will fall in love with my friend."

"Are you for real?" he exclaimed as he ran his fingers through his thick and wavy black hair. "How in heck would

Chapter 16 • The Greatest Gift of All

you know who I would like, and who I wouldn't, you don't even know me"!

Trying my best to convince him with an innuendo of curiosity before he went back to his car I asked, "Don't you even want to know who she is?"

"Okay...you've got my interest, who is your friend?"

Before I could tell him my friend's name, he caught me totally off guard by asking, "Is she the blonde that you're always walking with?"

Trying to stay nonchalant at this point was not easy since I realized that he knew exactly who I was talking about. With a big smile on my face, knowing half my work was already over, I happily replied, "Do you *know* my friend Jack?"

"Well no, not really," he said as he played with his car keys, "but, I have seen her at bingo a few times."

Still trying to maintain my calm composure I confirmed his guess. "Yes, that is my friend Helen."

Before I could say another word he added for good measure, "I've actually seen her at the bowling alley as well."

"Oh that's her for sure." We both knew we weren't talking about two different people. My next remark was nothing more than sheer small talk simply to prepare him for the next question. Somehow, the conversation was fast becoming effortless.

"Have you by any chance ever talked to her?"

He smiled, as if to say, "I thought you would never ask."

"No, I haven't."

This of course was music to my ears and I wasted no time asking, "Would you like to meet my friend now—since you already know who she is?"

Looking at me straight-up he said, "Maybe someday."

"Maybe someday!" I repeated, with unrestrained surprise.

"Yeah, maybe someday."

Searching for the right words once again, I soldiered on with, "Well, I think you should meet her sooner than later, because…well…you see…umm, there is something I should tell you about her."

Jack's face instantly appeared puzzled. I was hoping some of this, at least, could be attributed to intrigue. His overall body language seemed to say, *Continue, this is getting more interesting by the minute,* but he never said a word, he just waited for me to fess-up with whatever it was I had to tell him. Wiping the sweat from my brow, I remembered that he had in fact seen her at least a couple of times before, so this would work to my advantage. I decided to just state the facts as simply as I could, and my resolve to do so, seemed to make things a whole lot easier.

"My friend's name is Helen, and she is engaged to be married in three weeks."

Before I got any further this poor baffled man put both his hands up in the air saying, "Hold it, hold it. There is something you might want to know about me, and that is this; I will not get involved with a married, engaged, or any other woman who is in a relationship. And why, if your friend is engaged, are you trying to set me up with her?"

"Well that is another story, but the cause is noble. A legitimate one, but one which I can't quite explain right now," I said, suddenly realizing I had to go to another extreme. I had to take this bull-by-the-horns so to speak, otherwise he'd drive away and leave me dangling in the dust. Instantly, I got the idea to invite him to bingo and sit with us the coming Sunday night.

Chapter 16 • The Greatest Gift of All

"Do you ever go to BINGO on Sunday nights I offered, "My friend and I go to bingo every Sunday night, at the St Edmonds Church Bingo Hall. Meet us there, and I will arrange for you to sit with us. I can introduce you to her. How does that sound Jack?"

Looking at me as though I was completely wacko he stated, "Well, I happen to go to bingo at the same place on Sunday nights and, I've seen your friend there with an older man. I've always presumed he is her father. But, I have never seen you there."

Before he could say another word I cut in with, "Then I will save you a seat. Come early if you can Jack, okay?"

"If I go, I might see you there, he said with a little grin, which I knew meant he was convinced to go. He sounded reluctant, yet obviously intrigued by the whole thing.

As he opened the door of his gleaming, royal blue Chevy, and lowered himself into the driver's seat, I had an instant flash-vision of my friend sitting right there beside him! I was in a trance with this clear vision for several seconds. How could anyone *not* see this couple together I thought, as I pondered the fortuitous-looking prospects for the two of them.

Jack started the motor and it turned over instantly with a deep, low growl. He let the V-8 rumble a bit before putting the big blue beast into gear saying with a smile, "See you later"

Waving goodbye, but still somewhat in a daze, I watched the classic Chevy pull out of its parking spot, shift into second-gear and then disappear into a yellow-gold setting sun. It was a dramatic sight to behold. It was also a vision that has been etched in my memory since childhood. I had a very strong feeling that this young, good looking man—

whom I had just randomly met on the street—was about to change some peoples lives forever. Of course, he didn't even know it. How could he?

Needless to say, I felt this great feeling of accomplishment, knowing that I just set up a date for my girlfriend. But, the reality was that I still had to find a way to tell her that she had to go to bingo with me that Sunday night and, without her fiancé! I instinctively realized this was not going to be so easy since every minute she wasn't working was spent with her fiancé .

I felt like a school kid again, trotting down the sidewalk, with a skip to every step. I was smiling and talking to my angels the entire way, thanking them for helping me pull this match-making thing off, and for making sure I met the man that was going to play a big roll in my friend's life. The life that she would never know if she married the wrong man.

That night I lay awake in my bed looking for ideas, asking my angels, "How do I make my friend realize she is on course for making a colossal mistake? How do I tell her that I had a vision of her with a man I just met? How do I tell her, that she will break-up with her fiancé? Please tell me *how* to tell her!"

The next thing I knew, the sun shone through my sheer curtains and landed upon me, warming my face. This sliver of sunrise and the cheerful chirping sounds of robins were telling me it was morning. The smell of freshly brewed dark roast coffee was enough to get anyone out of bed, but for some reason, I wanted to just lay there contemplating things, taking in all the events that had happened the day before. Then, and sounding as if from miles away, I heard the phone ring. This was followed by my brother Nat yelling my name. He was calling me as loud as he could

Chapter 16 • *The Greatest Gift of All*

from the bottom of the staircase, "Mary, It's Helen on the line for you" His voice boomed throughout the house, and I jumped to my feet, almost tripping over them.

"I'm here, upstairs, I'll be there in a minute." I said, still wondering how I was going to find the words to tell Helen, that she had to go to bingo with me Sunday night.

"Hi Helen, I said, clearing my voice, I was going to call you today. I met this really nice guy yesterday and I just know you would really like him. He is very handsome and quite charming. He has a very unique voice and way about him. I'd guess him at about twenty-five or so. You may have seen him already, he drives that big blue Chevy Impala around town...hello...Helen...are you still there?"

"Yes I'm here," came back a flat-toned answer, "and as much as I would love to meet your new friend it will be impossible this Sunday. We have a birthday party to go to."

Suddenly I felt a mild, but steady rush of panic. I of course knew that the "we" in her sentence meant her *and* her fiancé. I was worried I'd become hysterical trying to convince her. I began with some basic pleading, saying, "Oh but you don't understand. You see, he is not *my* new friend, well that is, he is, but not really if you know what I mean."

"What on earth are you talking about?" Helen replied, dumbfounded.

"You're not making any sense. Is everything okay?"

"Well," I said, "I'm not going to beat around the bush, Helen. I met the man you are going to marry!"

"Now you're really not making any sense. Have you completely forgotten that I am engaged to be married in three weeks?"

"I know that," I said, "but I cannot see you marrying him. He just won't be your husband."

"Where did you get such a crazy notion?" she barked in my ear, "I am going to be getting married to the man I am engaged to, plain and simple."

Trying to deep breathe, and almost choking on my unrehearsed words, I stayed adamant to my conviction. "No, you won't be marrying Dave, Helen. I'm sorry, but you just have to believe me."

"Why are you trying to sabotage my wedding plans?" Her voice began getting louder. She sounded as upset as a wet hen, and I couldn't blame her for being so.

"Well I can't explain on the phone Helen. All I want you to promise me is that you and I go to bingo at the church hall this Sunday night." Not waiting for an answer, I continued with, "We have to go with your dad only. I'll pick our lucky seats and I will explain more about everything when we get there. Hello...hello, are you still there Helen? Helen?..."

I suddenly realized the line was dead. Helen had hungup on me because she didn't want to hear any more of this absurd nonsense. Quite honestly, if the shoe was on the other foot, I likely would have done the same thing. I poured myself a tea and calmed myself down for a few minutes before calling her back, begging her not to hangup until she listened to what I had to say. When I heard, "Okay, I'm listening," I knew I could state my case and save her from making the biggest mistake of her life.

From this crucial victory I took a big sigh of relief, feeling that I had just defied the odds by convincing my best-friend to do something she didn't have confidence, or belief in. Little did I know that the hardest part of this looming disaster was just around the corner, and I was right in the middle of it, again, as always..

Chapter 16 • *The Greatest Gift of All*

Sunday night came along faster than I had anticipated and I found myself hoping that the man I wanted to match-up with Helen was going to come through the swinging doors. I kept looking at the big clock and watching the entrance. I started getting nervous—worrying that Jack might not appear. Finally, the voice I recognized from hearing only once in a street conversation was booming across the room from where he was paying for his admission. I quickly went over to greet him before he could get lost in the crowd.

"Hi Jack, how are you doing?" I said, as I wove my way through the crowd of anxious bingo players. Before he had a chance to answer, I said, "Would you like to join my friend and I this evening?" Knowing his answer was going to be yes, I added, "I'm so looking forward to introducing you to Helen, my best-friend."

Before I could ask another question, Jack looked across the room in the direction of Helen and her dad and, in that moment, their eyes met. Jack found his way to the table like a magnet to a piece of steel. With a big smile upon my face, I followed. The moment we reached them, I knew the introduction would be something special. That freeze-framed moment of positive energy and deep connection which unfolded before me, was one that everyone should experience at least once in their lifetime.

The sparks were flying between Jack and Helen all night long. It was as though there was no bingo game, for never before have I seen Helen miss numbers or forget what game she was playing. I knew instantly there would be no wedding in two weeks, not for Helen and her fiancé anyway.

The next day, after that exciting night of heavenly bliss, Helen called me. She was on cloud nine, but in a dilemma.

"Okay, Miss Matchmaker. Now what?" She exhaled into the phone.

"What do you mean exactly?" I asked dumbfoundedley.

"Well, first of all, my sister is having a shower for me tomorrow night; she has gone out of her way and, spared-no-expense. I really don't know what to do, but seeing how you're the instigator, I'm desperately hoping you have something in mind for the consequences."

This was the part which I wasn't looking forward to, yet, I knew I had to offer some kind of suggestions for my dear friend who was now in a dilemma because of me. It was the only decent thing to do of course, but it was harder to come up with a solution for her than I had thought it would be. Helen's voice at the other end of the line was bordering on sheer panic, and the questions just kept coming.

"What do I do now? Do I phone them all? Do I tell them at the shower, or do I just not show up?"

"You have to show up Helen. It would be way too insulting to your sister not to. Listen, don't panic, I will take care of it and call you back."

"What do you mean; you will *take care of it?*"

"Well," I said, "there is always a way. If I have to go to the shower and stand up in front of everyone, and make a speech about my intuition, then I guess that is what I will have to do."

"Well that is probably what you should do since that is the truth. We've always been taught to tell the whole truth and nothing but the truth, haven't we?"

The days zipped by and the next thing I knew, the event was upon us. The shower took place as it was originally planned. Normally I was too shy to walk into a room full of people I knew, let alone a room full of complete strangers, and actually talk about my intuitive abilities. But something came over me that day such as I've never experi-

Chapter 16 • *The Greatest Gift of All*

enced before. I kept hearing a little voice inside my head, saying, "You must help your friend, you can't let her make the biggest mistake of her life." And every time I prayed about it, or asked my spirit guides for help in case I was the one making the big mistake, I would get an uneasy feeling inside of me. My inner voice would take over, giving me not only clear messages but visions of the event, so clear that it was like watching a movie on television. I could see my best-friend marrying Jack, and I could see it all in detail. I could see the two of them exchanging rings and wedding vows, the confetti in their hair. I could see them sitting in the back seat of Jack's Impala after saying "I do!" These visions which were so beautiful, real, and clear, were without a doubt what gave me the nerve to do what I had to do next.

I waited until everyone was seated, then snuck in the back door. I knew that the happy sounds of laughter and joy were soon to be sounds of shock and disbelief, but this I couldn't help—I had to do the right thing for a friend. I walked into the living-room where a big green arm chair was strung out with streamers and balloons, waiting for the bride-to-be. About twenty women were sitting about the room chatting and laughing, and having what appeared to be a lovely time.

Instead of finding a seat, I just stood in the middle of the room. A few started to offer me a seat as though I couldn't find one of my own. I just smiled and said, "Oh no thanks, that's okay." The host of the shower, the bride's sister, wondered at this point what was going on but never asked any questions. I stood there looking around at all the decorations, the gifts, the flowers and the food. I took a big breath, pressing my palms together as if to start a prayer. The vision of Helen and Jack popped into my head again, and that did it for me. At that moment, the words came flying out of my mouth. They were words that I had not rehearsed or ever thought of before. It started with something like, "Hello everyone, I am a friend of Helen's."

"I fully realize she is engaged to be married to Dave in a couple of weeks, but I have a very important message for all of you here. I need—and more importantly Helen will need—everyone's support and understanding. Mostly though, she will need some compassion."

At that moment you could have heard a pin drop with the sudden silence that had fallen. I had everyone's full attention, and they were all wondering what this could possibly be about.

"Is something wrong with Helen?" a woman asked, sporting a frowny-face. Looking straight at her, I replied, "No, actually Helen is just fine. But, she is not going to be coming to the shower, because there is *not* going to be a wedding."

The silence suddenly turned to agitated resentment, even borderline anger. When I said, "There is *not* going to be any wedding," everyone cried out almost on cue.

"What? Why?""No Wedding" and, "You've got to be kidding." seemed to flak the airspace around me. The exasperated words came from mothers, grandmothers, sisters, neighbours and every future in-law. Some carried tearful overtones, some carried rude ones. Others were simply baffled. Fortunately for Helen, a few seemed genuinely compassionate. There was a kaleidoscope of remarks and emotions circling about, and they were not so easy to take while standing there.

For a moment or two, I felt as if it were all my fault. Those faces, the unopened gifts, the food, the decorations, not to mention the hard work and expense that went into

Chapter 16 • *The Greatest Gift of All*

it, hardly benefitted from my announcement. I quickly recovered from any feelings of guilt however, and realized that it was the message I was delivering which was in fact the greatest gift of all. That is, the gift of happiness and love for two people who were really meant to be together. And as long as I kept that firmly in mind, the sad faces were just faces, and they no longer made me feel guilty.

I felt bad for the people who came from out of town, and for those who spent considerable time planning the shower not to mention the wedding itself. My only words of comfort for all those people were; "Sometimes things are just not meant to be." With the finalization of that statement—and not wanting to listen to anymore negativity, see any more tears, or have any more questions thrown at me, I politely asked everyone to reclaim their gifts for 'next time' and to try to still enjoy the day. I then abruptly, but casually, made my exit from the living-room and out the back door.

A few weeks passed by and I soon discovered that Helen and Jack were not wasting any time. They knew they wanted to marry each other shortly after they met. They got engaged three months later, were married that same year, and now—thirty-eight years later—are still married with three beautiful children and two granddaughters who look a split-image of their grandpa.

Chapter 17

WHEN THE PATH IS CLEAR

Every so often I get someone coming through my door that I'd swear I have met before. We have all experienced déjà vu at one time or another in our lives, but for me it seems not an infrequent occurrence. I love it because for me it's like no-one is ever a stranger, they feel like family

On One such occasion of this happened to me in the spring of 1985. I was busy sewing a patchwork quilt and could hardly hear the door-bell over the sound of the sewing machine. When I finally heard it, I quickly ran down stairs wondering how long whoever it was, had been waiting on my porch. I opened the door and saw a middle-aged, very attractive well dressed women with gazing blue eyes.

She stood tall in front of me, and before I could say a word, she announced, "A friend of a friend told me you are a psychic reader. She gave me your name and address and I was just wondering how soon I could get a reading." As she stood there talking, I suddenly felt like I had met this woman before. And, the way she spoke made it feel even more that way.

Chapter 17 • *When the Path is Clear*

"Well now," I said, "I am not too busy today if you would like to come in now, seeing that you're already here."

"Oh my goodness, I can't believe you have time for me now," she replied excitedly as she stepped through the door and into the foyer.

Bizarrely, it felt as though I was about to have a visit with an old friend—one that I had known for years it seemed. I had an unmistakable sensation of knowing her background. From her kids' names and their lives, to her mother, father, and husband. Everything she talked about was all uncannily familiar to me. I felt so at home with this woman—who finally introduced herself as Louise—that particular day I decided not to use cards, or any other medium. I would just go by the messages I was already receiving. Her aura was beautiful, and very easy to read. I found myself wishing I had a paint brush and canvas to depict the essence of it while I was reading her. We sat in the sunroom where I had my indoor waterfall trickling away and, low in the background, soft flute music complemented my water feature. As she sat comfortably in my big arm chair, she wasted no time and clicked her cassette-recorder on, ready to catch every word on tape.

At almost the same moment, I had a vision of her with a very nice looking older man. He was standing beside her and looking rather dapper. "Who is George?" I asked, as I looked into her far-away blue eyes.

With a curious reaction to my question, she said, "I worked for a man named George."

"No," I said, shaking my head. "This man is not a man you worked for—he will be in your life one day. But at this time I see him taking care of a sick women."

"Oh my," she gasped.

"I feel pain in your left knee. You will be having surgery on it and I'm not seeing you back at work until six months afterwards."

Well, she didn't like the sound of that too much I must say, but she did still listen carefully to everything I had to say.

Smiling, I said, "You are one of the lucky ones, you won't have to go looking for a man."

Intrigued, she asked, "What do you mean exactly?"

"What I mean is, this man I see will actually come knocking on your door."

"Yah right," she laughed.

"I'm not kidding," I said, "I see this good looking available man intentionally calling on you." "He is clearing a path for you"

Clearing a path for me? Yes it is snowing and the ground is being swept and cleaned"

"When do you see me meeting this person"? She asked in anticipation.

Laughing and making a joke I said, "I guess when the path is clean for you and him, and then it will be the right time for both of you"

A puzzled look flashed across her face. "Who *is he*? Has he come to my house before? Do I know him?"

Taking a deep breath, and containing myself from laughing alongside Louise, I told her, "No you don't know him and, he has never come to your door before."

She pondered my last statement for a second or two and then asked, "I have another question."

Stopping her in mid-sentence I stated, "I know what you

Chapter 17 • When the Path is Clear

are going to ask, and the answer to that question is: this winter. In fact, I see snow falling the day he looks you up."

I continued getting messages for over half-an-hour and, there were a few she didn't exactly want to hear. Especially when I said, "He is married dedicated and his hands are tied"

With a dejected look clouding her otherwise clear blue eyes she said, "Well that leaves him out. I'm not getting involved with a married man."

Trying to rejuvenate her spirits I replied, "Don't rule him out, because at the time he comes into your life, he will be widowed."

"Well I can't wait forever merely hanging on the hope that this man might cross my path someday"

"You just have to be patient Louise. Have faith and confidence in the universe and your destiny. In other words, Believe in Miracles too because they really do happen"

"Okay, because you are so sure of all this, I will try my best."

"How old is he? Will we be together in our old age?"

I couldn't help but notice the sparkle in her vast blue eyes and, without missing a beat, I answered her straight-away.

"He is in his early to mid-fifties, but even so, he is still very handsome. Tall and slim, I see him as being a good dancer. He will make you feel as though you've known him all your life. But you must be patient as I said, because his hands are currently tied in a faithful relationship and he is quite dedicated to his wife. He will be widowed from her by the time you meet him and, yes, you will be together in your old age." Before she could say or ask anything else, I continued with, "He will be your friend, your mentor, and your partner, but you will not marry him."

"I won't?" she gasped.

"That's right, you won't, but the two of you will be fine with that decision," I said reassuring her. "The important thing is Louise, you will both be happy."

"Mmm, I sure like the sound of that!"

On the way out to her car she turned around to bid me good-bye. "I'm going to keep you posted on this. I will definitely let you know if I meet someone fitting the description. The funny thing is, I can't say as I've ever looked forward to winter!"

Louise called me the following November. I was getting out of the shower, and got to the phone just in time. I wasn't surprised to hear her voice on the other end of the line when I answered.

"Hi Mary, remember me? It's Louise! I sold my house, like you said I would, and I've decided to move into town. I haven't found a place yet, and I'm booked for knee surgery next month. Your predictions have been coming true, of that there is no doubt. The only thing that hasn't happened yet is the appearance of that wonderful man you mentioned. Where the heck is he anyway? Do you still see him—are his hands still tied?"

Laughing, I was happy and amused at the same time. "No," I said, "as a matter of fact his hands are tied no longer—he is a widower now. And, as I'm sure you've noticed, it's just started snowing these last few days. You will be meeting this man very soon I feel, and your move has something to do with him finding you. I see him shovelling snow from your new driveway, and making a path for you to walk on. I can even see a glimpse of him through your kitchen window."

"*Where* will I be moving to?" she asked with a glow in her eyes.

Chapter 17 • *When the Path is Clear*

"I see you near a little park and an elementary school, in a small rural community. It will be a familiar place too, one where you once played as a child."

"Hmm, where I played? Oh my gosh, I know exactly where that is. I drove past this area the other day, and guess what? There *was* a house for sale!"

"Well that is where you are going to be living," I said as I wrapped a towel around the top of my head. "Let me know when you get settled as I'd love to come and see your new place."

"You really are sure, aren't you?" she said, hoping to get even more of a confirmation from me. "I will definitely let you know when I get settled-in, and thank-you so much for listening to me and giving me such fascinating insight. At least I now know where I'm going to be living. I just knew I had to phone you today!"

"Well I'm glad you did Louise, and as much as I'd like to continue the conversation, I'm just getting out of the shower so let's talk again another day. Keep me posted on everything."

"Oh I will for sure. We'll get together as soon as I get moved in."

Before long I was invited for tea to her new address. As I had envisioned, there was a park and school only footsteps away from her front door. The elementary school was just across the street and was in fact the same one she had attended as a young girl. Upon arriving, I immediately noticed what a picture-perfect job she had done of setting up her new home. We sat for a long time just sipping tea and casually talking about how everything always happens for a reason. How sometimes we don't listen to our own heart, or believe in our own desires, intentions, and choices. We talked about all the things that most people only talk about as best friends. And, just as it was with the first visit with Louise at my house, it seemed as though we were the oldest of friends. Looking about her new home, it was very easy for me to see that she was indeed at the right place to meet this man, as I could visualize him sitting right there where we were sitting. I felt his presence to be very close, as if only next door.

"Louise," I exclaimed, "I'm picking up a man right next door. He is the one I mentioned. The man I predicted to be in your life. He is going to come knocking on your door." And clearing your walkway"

"Well, actually, that is one of the reasons I wanted you to come over, to see if you pick-up his energy. The reason I'm so curious is that you mentioned that I may catch a glimpse of a nice man through my kitchen window. Come here and look out this window. You can see his house clear-as-day from here."

As I looked out her kitchen window it was just like clockwork. He had just come out the back door and was getting into his car, a gorgeous, mint-condition, Cadillac Eldorado. We both let out a squeal of excitement because there he was, just as he was in my vision.

"He *is* tall *and* good looking—just like you said he would be. About my age too!" Louise announced happily. "But, don't you think all the ladies in the neighbourhood are probably after him? Heaven knows if he will even have any interest in me."

"You know what Louise, I feel he won't be looking for anyone for quite awhile anyway, What he will need is a few friends, and some companionship—not any kind of commitment."

She thought about what I had said for a moment and

Chapter 17 • When the Path is Clear

then, looking for guidance, asked, "Should I try to be a friend now? Or should I just wait?"

"Louise, I said sharply why not just start by introducing yourself, and by letting him know that if he needs anything, he has a reliable neighbour just next door"

"A woman I know down the street mentioned he hasn't gotten over his wife's passing yet, so I haven't really talked to him or anything yet"

" If you really are interested in him as a person, and as a possible companion, why don't you try and make him feel like he has a reliable neighbor right now. He needs to know people care at this time of need. Try bringing him a plate of food or a house-plant, and get acquainted with him. Don't be too anxious, nosey or pushy. And, be honest and straight forward with him—after all, you are his neighbour."

A few days later Louise rang my phone once again. This time to tell me her sad story.

"Mary, you won't believe my bad timing! I was just about to bring my neighbour a nice pot of my home-made soup, when I looked out the window and saw him getting into his car with another woman. I suddenly felt light-headed. Then I was enveloped within a haze of shock. I wanted to cry out. I reprimanded myself not long after, and since then I can't stop from wondering why I'm feeling so upset, when I don't even know this man. Perhaps worse, I keep looking out the window every half-hour or so to see if I can catch a fleeting glimpse of him, but I never do"

Attentively and politely, I listened to her story and did my best to try to calm her anxiety. "Louise, how do you know this person is not a good friend, relative, or daughter of his?"

"That is true, I must admit. I never gave that much

thought to be honest. You're right, it could very well be just as you say." A daughter or sister-in-law or relative"

After a few more minutes of catching up, and just before saying good-bye, I tried to instil some upbeat energy into her reasoning. "Louise, do yourself a favour and start focusing on more positive thoughts—like how happy you are to see this poor devastated man, who has just lost his partner, in the company of so many wonderful friends."

That night she emailed me a quick little note telling me how much she appreciated my positive thoughts and perspective. She went on to tell me that she had decided to be more positive about everything from here-on-in. In brackets, she wrote:

> "I spent all morning preparing a mouth-watering entree to bring over to my neighbour; my best-ever country stew. Of course, the thought never crossed my mind that he may not like stew, but no matter if he doesn't. As you well know, all I want to do is have an excuse to go over to his house and get acquainted and of course, to let him know that I am just next door in case he needs anything.
>
> Thanks again for everything.
>
> Sincerely, Louise.
>
> ps: I wonder if his name *is* George?"

A few months later while at home preparing supper for a group of people, the phone rang and it was none other than Louise.

"I have to tell you about the man who came knocking at my door. It was just like you said it would happen—that I wouldn't have to go out looking for him, that he would come to me, and sure enough, he did. I'm so thankful to you for telling me to buy this house, because if you hadn't, I'm sure I wouldn't have met such a wonderful man.

Chapter 17 • When the Path is Clear

"That's great Louise! How did it happen?"

"Well, let me tell you! This very nice looking man actually came and knocked on my door—just like you said he would. I opened it wide to greet him and he reached out his hand and introduced himself as George. I almost fainted, and I kid you not. The first thing he told me was that he loved the country stew I had left him. That was quickly followed up with an offer to shovel my driveway. I just knew this man was for me; he was so kind and had such a nice gentile smile.

"This is wonderful news Louise. I'm very, very happy for you!"

"This all would not have happened without your words of encouragement. I had a hunch that everything was going to go my way the moment I was peaking out the kitchen window one morning while washing dishes. I was watching George shovel a pathway through the snow for me, and I noticed that the path he was shoveling for me, was in the direction of his house. So, in effect, my path and his were actually joined together as one! And this, I really do love; I remembered at that moment how you always said, 'One day your paths will meet.' I never dreamed it would happen quite so literally!"

Fifteen years later, and they still live side-by-side. They never did marry, but their lifestyle is the envy of most middle aged couples. They are Snow Birds in the winter, where Florida is their second home, they golf five days a week and spend Spring and summer in the sunny Okanagan Valley. George spoils her rotten and you never see one without the other. Louise loves having a handyman around, who loves gardening, cooking, dancing, travelling and most of all one that lets her be herself. She says that she has become a more positive person now believing in herself and other people, and has discovered her spiritual side, which she never knew she had. They hold meditation classes at their home, which I have attended. They have a poster size picture of their back yard hanging above the fireplace. The picture is of the two sidewalks covered in snow, except the shoveled out path that leads from George's doorstep to Louise's door step. It read's "When the Path Is Clear"

Chapter 18

HAVE A LITTLE FAITH

I always love the outcome of a baby story, especially when the baby comes into the world against all odds. I loved it even more when I once predicted that the doctors were wrong and that the woman in question would indeed become pregnant. And, without any form of fertility treatment either; in vitro, artificial insemination, or any other way except by the natural fertilization of her husband.

On more than a few occasions, where I've had such clear visions of the woman pregnant, wearing a cotton maternity chemise and walking—or waddling in some instances—I have a hard time understanding why the woman herself can't believe it. In one such instance, a young woman in her mid-thirties by the name of Sherry came for a reading. She was tall and slender with a very athletic build. She was married for five years and had tried absolutely everything to get pregnant. I could tell straight-away that there was something pressing on her mind since at first, she wouldn't look me in the eye. She began by telling me that she was told by her Dr. after intensive testing that her and her two sisters had a hereditary condition which prevented them from having children of their own. As she sat in front of me explaining this rare genetic deficiency I suddenly saw a vision of her, and it was one in which she was clearly pregnant! I couldn't help but blurt out the details of what I was seeing, everything from her labour pains to the delivery itself. The degree of clarity and vividness of these visions truly amazed me.

"I see you wearing a light blue paisley print maternity smock— with big white pockets." I said, as I stared into space as if in a trance. "I am picking up the name of David—David and Robert."

And then, like a ray of sunshine, a big bright smile came across Sherry's face. And, she finally looked at me.

"Oh my God. My husband's name is Rob, short for Robert, and his father's name is Dave, short for David. We've always said that if we ever had a boy, we would name him Robert. I wish it was true—what you're seeing I mean. Wouldn't it be wonderful though? She asked with a sigh. My husband and I have always loved kids, but we have more or less adjusted to being alone. Having two German shepherd dogs—that are just like our kids—is no substitute, but it sure helps."

"Hey, hey, hey. Stop right there!" I said, "By talking as though you are never going to be pregnant you are telling your brain, and you're subconscious, that your dogs are all you are going to have. You must replace that negative talk with visions of you being pregnant' and delivering your very own baby."

I continued to talk about the new bundle of joy as if she was already holding this baby in her arms. I went on to tell her, "You will have two children who will look as different as day and night." It was then I noticed that Sherry was on the verge of crying, holding back some tears but not all of them. As she fumbled in her purse for some tissues, I handed her some of mine that were within reach.

Chapter Number • *Have a Little Faith*

"I'm sorry." Sherry mumbled, almost inaudibly. She then sat straight up in her chair and searched for her voice. "It's just that this is something I have always dreamed of. I've conditioned myself to put it out of my head because of my genetics. Believe me there is nothing I would love more than giving birth to my very own child. But... I know that it is only a dream at best. Genetic realities would have to be defied for such a miracle to happen for me."

"Well," I said, "prepare for genetic defiance then! I don't know about you, but I not only believe in miracles, I pray to my angels for miracles often and many of them have happened. In fact, so many of them have, that I've documented each one with dates and names to help keep them straight. I have always subconsciously realized that someday they will make for terrific reading—positive subject matter too. Intriguing, real-life stories people can feel good about. They're only archives now, but soon I will have them published as a recollection of sorts." And who knows Sherry your story just might be one of them, so you must keep in touch, as I always like to hear about baby stories, especially if they are against all odds"

"I believe in miracles too, it's not that I don't. I just never ever thought of one happening to me, is all.. "Are you ever wrong in your predictions?" She asked looking me square in the eye.

My answer was the one I give every time. "Yes, I've been wrong before, many times in fact. But, this is one of those times whereby I'm 99 percent certain about you having a baby"

Breathing deeply and looking as though she might faint, Sherry confided, "I didn't tell my husband my intentions in getting a psychic reading. He doesn't really believe in such things , but, nonetheless, I feel I should tell him what you have predicted for us—especially considering this wonderous little matter involves him too!"

"You're absolutely right," I said, as we both laughed at her dry sense of humour.

I blew out the flickering candle in the centre of my reading table. "Rob is entitled to fill his life with hope and optimism along with you at this time Sherry."

"I just hope I can convince him that you are for real and, how strongly you feel that we will have our own baby."

Walking her to the door I gave her a last minute pep-talk. "Think positive and learn to relax. Practice doing both. Love one another and do your best to keep stress out of your lives. Eat healthy and pray." At that she gave me a hug and we said our goodbyes. She promised to stay in touch.

It was several months later when I ran into Sherry and her husband Rob at the local super market. We noticed and recognized each another immediately and Sherry wasted no time introducing me to Robert as, "the psychic reader that sees us with our own children."

We laughed light-heartedly and kept our conversation simple until Rob piped up and said, "You know we have been trying even harder to get pregnant, even though the Dr's have said Sherry has a genetic disease" We have managed to keep stress out of our lives quite successfully, and we've been combining a nutritious diet with a litany of vitamins and super-foods from the local health-food store. We exercise everyday, and have done everything by the book for conceiving a child. But...I'm afraid to say, "No cigar yet! We have had disappointment after disappointment," he said as he shook his head and wiped his brow.

"It's hard for me to keep pretending we are going to be

Chapter Number • Have a Little Faith

parents someday, when most likely we won't be, Rob said as he gently put his arm around Sherry's shoulder. I guess it's because for years both Sherry and her sister have been told that they have a genetic disease and cannot and will not ever bear children. I know you are psychic, and you have said without a shadow of a doubt, that we are going to be parents of our very own children, but I'm willing to bet money that this time you're wrong."

Feeling like someone had just knocked the wind out of me; I managed to stay calm and collected. In a sympathetic tone, I gave him my reply. "I'm really sorry you feel that way Robert, because I can still see you both with your own child, you will be pushing a baby in these grocery carts just as sure as we are standing here. You just need to have a little faith. Faith in God, Miracles and in me wouldn't hurt either' I said laughing

Laughing and shaking his head, he turned away, pushing the grocery cart saying, "I don't think so. It appears this time you're wrong."

As I turned away myself, I could hear Sherry say under her breath, "You could have at least said we would *like* to believe you..."

It was the following Christmas when, in the middle of making gingerbread cookies with my little nieces, the phone rang, and we decided to let the call go to the answering machine due to the baking mess that was all about us. The moment I heard the voice of a girl cry out I recognized who it was.

"Hello, Merry Christmas. This is Sherry Campbell, You were right! You were right!   We have a baby" I wiped the cookie dough from my hands as quickly as I could on the nearest tea-towel, and reached for the phone.

"Hi Sherry—I'm here. How wonderful!" I added, with what must have been an obvious tone of surprise.

"I just wanted to tell you the good news. Isn't that great? We went to Africa and adopted a baby," she said, her voice still loud in the receiver.

Scratching my head, I replied, "How nice for you Sherry, and I'm sure for the baby too."

"You don't *sound* very thrilled," she said flatly, "I thought you'd be happy to hear our wonderful news. You don't see some misfortune or something do you?"

"Oh, goodness no, quite the opposite in fact. I see nothing but a healthy and happy baby but..." I guess I'm just baffled because you went to Africa to adopt a baby "

"But what?" she asked, with an undertone of worry still in her voice.

"Well, I have to tell you the truth, and that is, I still see you pregnant!"

"Could it be that maybe you're seeing someone else's pregnancy, someone resembling me perhaps. Genetics has decided for me from the beginning—I'm convinced of it. One cannot argue with one's DNA, you know."

Not wanting to continue with more redundant negativity, and knowing she had blocked my prediction out of her mind completely, I ended our conversation with, "Well, I wish you all the best with your new little bundle of joy and, from all of us here, we want to wish you a very Merry Christmas." Sherry thanked me and said she'd stay in touch. I hung up the phone shaking my head. Under my breath I was saying to myself, "Now that is going to be one busy mother!"

When my little neice asked, "Why is she going to be so busy, aren't all mothers busy with a new baby"? My reply

Chapter Number • Have a Little Faith

was simple and to the point, "Yes all mothers are always very busy with a new first baby, but they are very very busy when they have two new babies"

"Yeah like when a mother has twins, Right"? Laurie exclaimed, "Yeah just like when you have twins" I said, as I got my hands back in the cookie dough. Almost as instantly as our gingerbread cookies were shaping up, I could see a clear vision of two' of everything, from baby buggies to baby cribs.

The following summer I was not surprised to get the phone call I had been expecting for a while.

"I wish I would have believed you Mary! Now I know why you were trying to convince me to have patience. You said not to quit trying because sooner or later, I would be pregnant. You somehow knew that my kids would look as different as day and night. Well, that prediction could not have been more accurate. I don't know why I didn't believe you, and I am truly sorry if I hurt your feelings every time I said I couldn't believe you" My husband and I are still in shock to be honest."

"So, I take it this is Sherry, and you are now pregnant," I said laughing out loud with excitement.

"Yes it is, and yes I am! You said you could see me waddling along, well I'm not at that point yet, I'm only three months along, but have gained ten pounds already, so I'm sure I will be waddling along any old time now" In six months we will have two children less than one year old"

"Fantastic news Sherry! You always wanted your very own child and soon enough, you will have just that."

"My husband is now one of your biggest fans. And, because we didn't believe your prediction, he thinks that if the baby is a girl we should name her Faith."

"Well, my comment on that is, you will have a healthy little girl and, her name may very well be Faith." And… I said jokingly, if you have a boy call him Moses" because I'm sure when your husband heard you were pregnant, his first words were "Holy Moses"

Chapter 19

THE WINNERS

Many times throughout my years of psychic readings, coaching, mentoring, intuitive counselling, and even hairdressing, I have had many visions of people winning something. There have been visions ranging from everything; cars, trips, jewellery and money, gold medals and ribbons. But one occasion in particular always brings a smile to my face. It was the time when I saw a huge diamond ring sparkling away on the finger of a woman who had come for a reading.

It was obvious to me that this woman, Alice, was not a jewellery kind of person. She wore very stylish clothes yet wore no jewelry whatsoever. Even so, I kept seeing this big ol' diamond ring glittering away on her finger every time I glanced down at her left hand.

"I'm sorry for staring," I said with a smile, "but I keep seeing a big diamond ring on your left hand.

She reached out her hand to me, offering me a closer look. I took her hand in mine and, when I did, I could not only see this ring, I could almost feel it. Pointing to her ring-finger I announced, "This is where you will soon be wearing a big solitaire diamond ring."

Laughing she replied, "Well, I don't have money for rings, let alone diamond ones! And, my husband and I are separated now, so I can't see it at all. It is a beautiful thought though!"

"Actually Alice, it is not from your husband and you're not buying it either. You are going to be winning it!"

"Winning it?" she cried out. "You've got to be kidding me."

"No I'm not kidding you are—winning it."

"But I can't quite see how. I haven't entered any contests. In fact, I have never entered any kind of contest, because I can't see myself ever winning anything"

"Well," I offered, "there is always a first time."

"Hmm...a diamond ring you say."

I continued with her reading, picking up vibes on her life in general but nothing more regarding her winning this diamond ring. As I walked her to the door, she asked, "Do you think the diamond ring you are seeing is on my *daughter's* finger, because she is hoping for an engagement ring from her boyfriend"

Wiping my brow from the summers heat, I answered, "No, I see it on *your* finger, clearly too! *You* will be the lucky and happy woman who wins this diamond ring."

"I believe everything you've told me today because it was bang-on, but this bit about winning a diamond ring is just too far fetched for me. I have never ever won anything in my life. I'm just not a lucky person."

Well, let me tell you a little secret," I offered with a broad smile. "If you want to win something, you just have to tell yourself you are going' to win. Not maybe' might' should or could, but you will' win" Tell yourself you are a very

Chapter 19 • The Winners

lucky person! Convincing your subconscious that you are lucky will transcend to being lucky. It's the easiest way we can manifest things to happen. And, it actually works." I've proven that hundreds of times, as anyone in my family can tell you. But that would be another book"

That night I was cleaning up the kitchen when I noticed the box of dishwasher detergent I was holding had a picture of a big diamond ring on its front. I turned it around to see what it was all about and sure enough, it was a contest anyone could enter to win this big beautiful solitaire diamond ring. I stopped dead in my tracks in amazement because it was exactly like the ring I had just seen on Alice's finger in my vision. My heart began to race, because I knew this was the contest she simply had to enter but, how would I get in touch with her again not having her phone number or knowing her last name? I barely slept a wink that night. I spent most of the night praying as well as wracking my brain, trying to come up with a way in which to contact with her.

I finally got a bit of sleep after hearing the voices of my angels and spirit guides telling me after three in the morning; "It's way past your bedtime. Go to sleep, find her name tomorrow"

By the time I opened my eyes the sun was already beating in through the bedroom window, illuminating my entire room in a golden glow. The first thing on my mind was Alice. It was only moments later when I had another vision of the same big diamond ring—exactly like the one depicted on the dishwasher detergent box—on her finger. That just did it for me, and I knew then this was a vision that was going to come to pass, whether she was the unluckiest person in the world or not.

I jumped out of bed, and wasted no time getting to the

kitchen. I grabbed the box and tore off the picture of the ring so that I could tape it to my fridge. This facilitated my ability to pick up on the details of winning it even faster. As far as I was concerned, it was as though she had already won it, such was the realism of the visions I was having. I knew this was not a contest for me, it was her time and her luck, but I just had to get in touch with her.

It wasn't twenty minutes later when, sipping my first cup of coffee, the phone rang. I instantly had the feeling it was going to be Alice and I wasn't wrong. I also knew that she was about to tell me she was going to enter a contest.

"Good morning Mary, sorry if I called too early, but I am so excited. I need to tell you something."

Smiling, and taking another sip of coffee, I said, "You sound as happy as a clam, what happened?"

"You told me a few weeks ago that you saw me winning a diamond ring, and I told you I thought I was the unluckiest person in the world. Well, I found a contest on my box of dishwasher detergent this morning—it's for a beautiful solitaire diamond ring! Now don't you think that is quite a coincidence, considering what you've told me?

Laughing and feeling the happy vibes of her energy and excitement along with her, I said, "You will be winning this contest Alice, I'm sure of it."

"I have a feeling I might win it too, which is unusual for me."

"I hope you are going to be more positive than that. You have to say you *are* going to win that ring—not might."

"Well the reason why I feel that I might', is because I bought fifteen boxes of the detergent to have a better chance at the contest."

Laughing I said, "But you didn't need to buy fifteen box-

Chapter 19 • The Winners

es to have a better chance, because you will be winning regardless—one box, or a thousand boxes."

Over the following days, every time I went to the super market, I checked out the dishwasher detergent isle, just to see how many contest boxes were left. And sure enough, the other day, not only did I not see the diamond ring on the new boxes, but I knew that the Name Alice was going to be the name of the winner."

Several weeks went by and every night I picked up my dishwasher detergent to start the dishwasher, I had the same feeling as always, Alice was winning the Diamond ring, and she would be phoning to tell me all about it.

I wish I had a tape recorder to tape her phone call that announced her big win. She was ecstatic to say the least, and had everyone around her in disbelief.

"I won the ring. I won the ring! They just called to inform me I was the lucky winner. I'm still in shock. I can't believe I actually won something!"

These were the words I was hearing at the other end of the line, as she panted and caught her breath between sentences. I listened to this woman with a great sense of self satisfaction, knowing that only months before, she was so certain, she couldn't win anything, even if her life depended on it.

I had another experience quite similar to this one the following year, when a woman by the name of Kathy wanted her cards read. She was in her late forties, tall, slender and attractive. She owned her own thriving beauty salon in our community where she employed several well known hairdressers.

I began her reading the same way as I always do with a candle burning, soft music playing, and water trickling from my water feature alongside my fig tree. As tranquil as the surroundings were, she became agitated not long after we sat down. She seemed to want to say something, so I asked, "Is there something you want to tell me?"

"Umm, well...yes, kind of..."

"I know," I said, "You are one of the millions of people who don't really believe in psychic predictions, right?"

"How did you guess?" She laughed.

"Just a wild guess," I replied, as I poured her a glass of water. "You will change your mind once I start reading, so just relax, and enjoy this time."

Sitting back in her chair, she closed her eyes and took a deep breath, telling me "I'm ready for whatever you tell me." And with those encouraging words, I got started with her reading.

It was all going very well, with Kathy writing down my messages as fast as she could scribble on her notepad. It was only minutes into her reading when I told her, "You will be winning a trip." I see you sitting on the white sandy beaches of Hawaii, wearing a lei around your neck"

How wonderful! My husband and I are overdue for a much needed vacation, and we keep talking about going to Hawaii.

Her scribbling came to a dead-stop when I said, "Your husband will not be going with you."

"Well then I won't be going to Hawaii," she blurted, "because I can't see myself ever going without my husband on such a trip, Las Vegas... maybe, but not Hawaii."

Choosing to ignore her comment, I continued to stay focused on my visions. I continued to give her the messages about selling her business, driving a silver sports car, mov-

Chapter 19 • The Winners

ing away to another province, all of which she wrote down with enthusiasm.

"You are going to Hawaii with two other girls," I announced. Before I could say another word she looked up from her notes, and stared straight into my eyes with a frowny-face I'll never forget, telling me, "I won't write that one down because I just know it won't be happening. I seldom go anywhere without my husband, and never on a holiday such as Hawaii"

"I wouldn't be too sure about that if I were you, because you would be surprised what happens when one least expects it." And I see it as clear as you sitting in front of me, Oh and don't bother packing a bikini, because you will be buying two of them at the big market place in Honolulu" I said trying to convince her of my vision. She didn't see any humor in my statement, and as the reading came to a close Kathy's single question was, "How do I win this trip to Hawaii?"

My answer was, "It has something to do with a donation or fund-raiser."

Shrugging her shoulder, she replied, "Well if I *did* win anything to do with a fundraiser, my husband would be a big part of it, so, it's likely he would be coming, If I did win a trip any where"

I handed Kathy her coat, telling her, "Nope, your husband will *not* be going with you to Hawaii!"

As I closed the door behind her, I could sense her not being happy with the way I was so persistent about her husband not going with her, but when my intuition and inner voice gives me a strong message, such as this one was, I have to deliver it without any frills, even if the person doesn't always like to hear it.

The next time I heard from Kathy, she was up on cloud nine. Talking to her over the phone, I could hardly understand what she was saying.

"You were right! I won! I can't quite believe it yet," she told me, yelling into my ear.

"How exciting for you!" I said, chuckling to myself. "How did you win?"

"Well, because I own a business," she explained, "I was given the opportunity to enter a contest with other business owners in the community. My Beauty Shop actually won the trip! So I have to go with one of the employee's. So one of my hairdressers and I are going to Hawaii just like you said. The whole thing is simply amazing and, so are you!"

I thanked her for the call and thought to myself, *Hmm... funny how fast a person can become a believer.*

I've only had a vision of a 'Hawaii win' twice in my career as a psychic; the other time was really quite comical to say the least. This was once again a woman, very attractive, energetic, talented, and creative. She was in her mid thirties and her name is Cherise. Best of all, she was a strong believer in not only my gifts as a psychic, but in herself, and the powers of the universe. She had an inherent understanding of what people are capable of. We often talked about omens, miracles and fate, and how everything happens for a reason. Certainly, this was another one of those occasions.

It was a warm summer day when Cherise and I had just sat down with a cup of tea, which was her preference over tarot cards. I was in the middle of her reading, when all of a sudden I heard her full name loud and clear, and said right out of the blue, "You are going to be winning a trip.

Chapter 19 • The Winners

I see you sitting under a palm tree with an umbrella drink in your hand! You're wearing an over-sized straw sun-hat. I can see the big Island of Hawaii, and even Maui, and Kauai."

"Oh my gosh, I would love to go to Hawaii, and bask in the sun. It would be a dream come true, I'm getting excited just thinking about it. When do you see me going?"

It came to me instantly, "Three months."

"How do I get an entry form?"

Laughing I said, "I don't see an entry form. I know this sounds ridiculous, but I don't. I just know you are winning a trip to Hawaii within three months." I was of course baffled at the time, since I couldn't imagine how anyone could win a trip without filling out an entry form of some kind. Hmm I'm beginning to wonder myself, how will she win if she doesn't fill a form out"? This is weird, to say the least, but I can't say there is a form if I don't see one, and I really didn't see one at all.

As it turned out, a few days later, I got a phone call from Cherise telling me that she was driving down the highway with her radio on, when she heard a contest mentioned on-air. If you were the ninth caller, you could be a winner of a trip to Hawaii.

"Mary, you can imagine what was going through my head. My heart skipped a beat and I quickly pulled off the road to dial the number they announced. Would you believe I was the ninth caller? They answered the phone with, 'You are the ninth caller! Congratulations, you have the possibility of winning a trip to Hawaii!' I thought I *was* the winner of the trip, but I didn't know how the contest worked. After you seeing me win a trip to Hawaii, all I could think about was that I had won the trip. I was actually on the air live hearing that I was the ninth caller." After I hung up it suddenly hit me that this is the way I am going to win the trip to Hawaii. I was hysterical, well, you can imagine how I felt when the voice on the line said in a very serious tone, 'I'm sorry, but you are not a confirmed winner yet', because the ninth caller every day for another week has the opportunity to have their name in the barrel, and at week's end, we will draw the lucky name, and that is who will win the trip to Hawaii.' I sighed with relief when they told me my name would go into the barrel, because I know with every cell in my body that I am going to win the trip. I can feel it really strongly, and I just know that they will be announcing my name over the air, and in the paper as the winner."

"That's the spirit Cherise! You are such a positive person and that is why you will be the winner. I'm very confident for you because of your positivity and even more so because we both feel it."

A week later I was basking in the sun on one of our local beaches, when someone's radio was blaring away, and I heard the station announce the winner of the trip to Hawaii, listening and smiling I knew by the time I got home there would be a message on my answering machine telling me the great news.

This was certainly one of those days when you feel good about the gift you share with others, to make their life a happier place. It was one of those phone messages I never erased for a couple weeks, just to listen to that happy ecstatic voice of another lucky winner.

Chapter 20

NORTH TO ALASKA

The first time I ever heard the words *Google* Earth I was dumbfounded. These were two words I had never before heard since—at the time—I had no computer, cell phone, printer, fax machine or any other modern electronics. So, imagine my amazement when a perfect stranger from Alaska found me and my residence just by knowing my name. When I asked him how on earth he found me from way up in Alaska he smiled, and told me, "Oh, quite easily actually."

He then pulled out a little map from his wallet depicting my subdivision. Looking stunned I'm sure, and feeling like I had been lost in a time capsule, I reached out to take it from him. *This is too unnerving,* I thought to myself.

"I don't know a lot about computers," Jim said, "but I do know that if I want to find someone, I just have to type in their name and city and up comes their address with a map, and I heard about you from a man whom you read a few years ago"

I was in awe of this new technology. I handed him back the map shaking my head and laughing, "I guess I'd better get with the program, and find myself a computer and go back to school"!

Not long after this reading I had the privilege of meeting many more families from Alaska as well as the surrounding areas of the Yukon Territory. All of which have become very good friends since. The one that I see most often is Dwayne—Jim's son—the man who first found me with the internet map. Dwayne is tall, good looking, and blue-eyed with blonde hair. He is soft spoken, friendly, and easy to talk to with a great sense of humor. The first time I met him was in 2003. He also found me using his dad's internet map, and it was going to be his very first psychic reading.

Surprisingly, he was not the least bit nervous or hesitant. Instead, he was excited and anxious to find out all he could about his life and where I could see it going. We no sooner got comfortable in my reading room when I had a vision of a huge big, white fish. And I'm not just talking regular 'big' either. No, this was more like gigantic. Whale-size in fact! I took a long deep breath and thought to myself, *how can this be possible, a fish bigger than this young fellow who stands at least five-foot-ten.*

"I'm seeing you standing beside a huge, fat gigantic size fish Dwayne." Expecting him to laugh, I continued with, "It's hanging from a big hook beside you. There is a post card effect to it." I said, as I looked at his reaction, still amazed at what I was seeing.

Dwayne's mouth opened, and his jaw dropped. "This is amazing! You're not going to believe this," he exclaimed, as he jumped out of his chair. "I need to run out to my truck for something I want to show you. It is going to blow you away, just wait here I'll be right back"!

Curious as to what exactly he was referring to, I replied, "I can't wait to see what it is." Dwayne hurried down the hall and out the front door, almost bashing into it in the process.

Chapter 20 • North to Alaska

"This is going to be interesting," I said to myself as I sat there waiting to see what it was that had caused him such immediate excitement. Sitting there, I had another vision of him giving me a gift. I no sooner had the thought out of my head when Dwayne jogged back into the house and presented me with a photograph of him. He was standing beside a huge white halibut. He had just caught the gargantuan fish on an excursion off Vancouver Island a few days earlier, which weighed in at 150 pounds, just under his weight but the halibut won outright in length versus Dwanye's height. Remarkably, it was pretty much exactly what I had just seen in my vision. He mentioned he had a professional photographer capture the moment, and it looked it. The impressive picture would not be out of place on a postcard just as I had envisioned. I had never seen a fish quite that big before—one that someone had caught that is. It was only the day before when he had it filleted and packed in ice for his journey home. Dwanye took the photo out of my hand and replaced it with a king-size package of fresh halibut steaks! I shook my head in happy amazement, as I looked into his big travel freezer that he had rigged up in the camper of his big truck. "Man you learn something every day" I said, as I looked on in sheer amazement, at all the frozen packages of beautiful white halibut.

"What a unique and generous gift Dwayne, I said as I took this big frozen package from him. My goodness it feels like it weighs 20lbs. I really love halibut, it's my favorite fish, but I have to admit though, I've never seen such enormous big packages of it, I will savor every mouthful for a week I'm sure"

"I'm glad you like Halibut because I can bring you more of it every time we come through. I just thought you would be amazed to see this picture and the fish that was in your vision"

When we finally got back to his reading it seemed as though he was no longer a stranger. This naturally added to the casualness of the atmosphere and, even better, enhanced the clarity of the visions I was picking up. Like the big dump-trucks I suddenly saw him buying. I could see good times ahead for what looked like a sand or gravel business, with big yellow heavy, noisy machinery, coming and going on old logging roads in the middle of no-where. A smile and a sigh of relief suddenly came across his face, when I could see him sitting behind the wheel getting lots of work. A big beautiful dog—a Husky, that will be just like your room mate, and will go everywhere with you, he will temporarily be your company on long lonely nights" As fast as I was seeing these images, Dwayne was scribbling them down on a note pad from his pocket.

Dwayne appeared genuinely happy with his very first reading and seemed impressed with my predictions. I asked him if there was anything in particular on his mind before wrapping up the session.

"Well, I was wondering when, or if you see a girlfriend in my future."

"Not right away, in fact not for at least two years"

"Two years"! …Hmm.. "That long huh"?

"It's not really that long, some people have to wait a lifetime"

"That's true I guess, I just thought that maybe.. I would meet someone sooner than two years"

"I see her living in another province, far away—like half-way across Canada."

"Half-way across Canada!" he gasped. "But…how will I ever meet her? I don't travel anywhere across Canada."

"You won't need to travel across Canada, or anywhere for that matter, because one day she will live in your city."

Chapter 20 • North to Alaska

"Really?" he queried curiously. "I sure hope you're right. I don't want to meet the wrong person just because I'm getting older, and perhaps more impatient as a result. To be honest, I would rather wait for the right one."

Smiling, and giving him one of my famous warm touches, I said, "Believe me Dwayne, she will be the right one. I see you marrying this girl and, having a little boy one day, he will be a carbon copy of you"

"I love kids! How clearly do you see this?"

"You know Dwayne," I said with a motherly tone, "you have to be patient, because I don't see her just around the corner."

"Oh no," he cried out, "it's sounding like I might be an old man first!"

"No, you won't be an old man, far from it in fact. You will be in your early thirties, and that my friend is still very young."

As he clicked his pen and started to fold up his papers, he contentedly stated, "Well, now that I know I will be meeting the right girl for all the right reasons, I feel a lot better."

"Yes, you will have that part of your life fulfilled one day," I told him with confidence. "She will be worth waiting for Dwayne, I can tell you that."

We ended the reading on this happy note and exchanged phone numbers and mailing addresses. I again thanked him for the much appreciated gift of halibut steaks, and walked him outside to his big black truck. It was as though he was a relative or very close friend, because normally I say goodbye at the door. Somehow this client was different, felt more like a son than a client.

We kept in touch, and every year since then Dwayne

would come down from the Yukon Territory to see me for a reading session. He was as curious as a monkey, wanting to find out if the woman of his dreams was any closer or, if she was going to show up at all. Well, two years went by and it was session number four. I remember we were both left wondering where-oh-where this girl might be. To my happy surprise, I picked up a name while doing my hair one morning.

It was quite unusual because I heard this name so loud and clear, almost as if someone was hollering it in my ears. *How exciting*, I thought. I almost shouted out loud. Talking to myself in front of the mirror, I savoured the discovery. "This is Dwayne's girl; it's her name alright, I'm sure of it! I have to call him right away with this news!"

I went to my address book in a panic, as if her name would vanish from memory if I didn't hurry. While searching for Dwayne's number, I was thinking how happy he was going to be having at least a name—her name. To finally know the first name of the girl he will soon marry. I could hardly catch my breath, and as I fumbled through my address book my phone started ringing. There was something about the timing, even the tone of the ring. It was this, along with my intuition, just like her name, that would always tell me who is calling. I pretty much knew it was going to be Dwayne. Sure enough, it was.

Hi Mary, this is Dwayne. I know I'm about half a year early, but I'm seeing a naturopath in the South Okanagan next month. I was wondering if it would be okay if I stopped by for another reading on the way through Vernon?"

Hardly giving him time to finish what he was saying, I jumped in with, "Dwayne, I see her name!"

"Whose name?" he asked, with instant curiosity.

Chapter 20 • North to Alaska

"The girl you are going to meet and marry! Her name is Jennifer. So now you know."

"Wow!"

"Write it down," I suggested.

"Oh I won't forget it, but I am writing it down" I don't know anyone with that name right now, and I know pretty much everyone in Stewart, my little town, and I haven't met anyone with that name, not yet anyway"

"I see a white and green, out of province license plate. In fact, you will see the license plate before you see her. She is going to be relocating to work in your community. It's either a hospital or health clinic, I'm not quite sure. A sterile setting all around her in any case but, she is not a nurse. I see her immediate environment as clerical. Not only that, I see your life changing completely within three months. You're going to be a busy young man," I said with a big smile, "but don't worry, it will be a 'happy' kind of busy! Dwayne this is the girl, I'm telling you!" It was then I realized there was silence on the other end of the line. "Are you there Dwayne?"

"Oh you bet I'm here. I'm in shock, but I'm still here. I can't wait to come down for another reading after hearing this."

"Well I have more good news for you. When I see you next time, it won't be for the reading you're thinking of."

"And why not?" he asked blankly.

Laughing out loud and feeling excited for him, I answered with, "Because by the time I see you again, you will have already met her. You will be coming to tell me your love-at-first-sight story!"

"You continue to amaze me Mary. I can actually feel it too. I'm starting to believe she really *is* just around the corner."

Needless to say, I wasn't too surprised when I got a call from my northern friend less than a week later.

"Hi Mary, this is Dwayne from the Yukon. Do you have time to talk?"

"Yes of course, I always have time to talk." Smiling happily, I knew that I wouldn't need to do much talking. I got myself comfortable and ready to listen to another unique love story.

"Great, because I have exciting news." Dwayne's upbeat voice revealed the story to come, or at least the essence of it, and I found myself looking forward to hearing the details. "Well," he started, "you won't be too surprised to hear that I have finally met the girl you always said I was going to meet. And, her name really is Jennifer—just like you said it would be. In fact, it's even spelled the same way!"

"Go on," I said curiously.

"I spotted a Chevy with Ontario plates in the parking lot of a pub one night while I was out with some friends. It was a nice looking white Monte Carlo. I figured I had nothing to lose so I began looking around for the driver. I looked near everywhere but turned up nothing. Strangely enough though, I had this strong feeling that this new car in town belonged to the girl you've been talking about these last five years—the one I am destined to marry. Sure enough, the next day I found the same car in the same parking lot, and this time I was determined to find out who the owner was. I went into the pub trying not to look too obvious. I began scanning the place for a new, unfamiliar face. It was then that I glanced over to a table where there was a group of five people. Suddenly, I saw the face that stopped me dead on my feet. I was instantly drawn to her like a magnet. Funny, thinking about it now, because I've never before believed in love-at-first-sight, but this really

Chapter 20 • North to Alaska

and truly was. The magical thing was that she noticed me. She looked at me as if she knew me, and from that moment on, we couldn't stop looking at one another. It was quite the extraordinary experience and I didn't want the moment to end. I was up in the clouds, let me tell you. I knew the minute I laid my eyes on her—combined with the way she looked back at me—that it was her, the girl with the out of province plates. I also knew it was the girl I had been looking for my whole life. Are you still there Mary?"

"Oh yes, I'm still here, I said, "I love hearing these details Dwayne, keep talking."

"Well, you said I would fall instantly in love with this girl, and I have definitely done that! You told me she would be working in a hospital setting if not exactly in the capacity of a nurse. Well, she has a nursing degree, but she's working at the hospital as a nursing clerk—that makes you 'bang-on right' again! I wanted you to know that so far everything has happened exactly the way you said it would."

"Thank-you so much for telling me your beautiful story Dwayne," I said. "Now, do you want me to tell you what I see next?" Before he could answer my question, I announced with a grin, "I'm picking up a baby, a boy. I see three number 9's and a name too—a biblical name. I'm getting strong vibes for the name Matthew. He will be a big baby, and cuddly too. I see big blue eyes, and long eye lashes."

"You really see a boy huh? Well that is great because I have always dreamed of someday having a little boy to go fishing with; to carry on the tradition I have with my dad."

We soon ended the conversation and said our goodbyes along with the usual, keep-in-touch promise.

Another year was barely over when the next phone

call came from Dwayne. This time, it was not the flurry of questions as it had been the past years. Instead it was exciting news about the baby's birth announcement. Of course, it never really surprised me, and I was delighted to hear about it.

"Guess what Mary—we're parents now! We had a baby 9 months after my last reading and, just as you guessed, it was a boy. You'll be happy to know we named him Matthew. And, regarding your 9s, there's more; he weighed 9 pounds and was born on the 9th day of the 9th month. We're looking forward to bringing him over one of these days so you can hold him and see those big blue eyes and long lashes you so accurately predicted."

Chapter 21

WORST CASE SCENARIO

I thought I had heard and seen it all in my forty years of intuitive reading and taping into peoples psyches. Everything from relationships that were made in heaven to ones that ended on the honeymoon. Babies that were born to women who were sterile, violent tempers that turned gentle, husbands or wives that were willing to lose everything for a new love affair, winning the lottery with numbers from a reading, to the thousands of other intriguing, life changing stories that melt one's heart and warm one's soul.

However this next story is certainly proof that a psychic's life is never dull, always entertaining and, doesn't always warm your soul.

It was a hot summer day in July, 2005 and I was vacationing on Vancouver Island, in a quaint little town called Qualicum Beach. It was a trip I had been looking forward to for more than six months. I arrived with everything I needed for a week of sunbathing, relaxing, writing, and touring around the island. I was happily getting relaxed and tanned on the beach one day while writing some chapters for my book *Finding Happiness without Children*, when I heard the faint sound of my cell phone ringing in my stuffed to the brim beach bag. Had the sound of the crashing harbour waves been any louder than they were, it's quite likely I wouldn't have heard it at all. Rummaging through my bag was not unlike looking for a needle in a hay stack, finding it full of sand, coconut oil, note-pads and pens, paperbacks and pamphlets. I found it soon enough and quickly flipped it open to hear a loud and anxious German accented voice asking, "Ease dis dee psychic lady?"

Putting my finger in one ear, trying to hear her more clearly with the other, I replied, "Yes it is, Who am I speaking to?" I asked, as sand was blowing in my face as a result of the breeze and a couple of kids shaking their towels in my direction.

"My name ease Luta, I need you tell me somesing dis day," she demanded. Spitting sand from between my teeth, I was naturally curious of the time-sensitivity. "Can you come to me dis day?"

Is she for real? I found myself thinking. *Today?* It wasn't easy understanding her broken English and the accompanying heavy German accent made it even more difficult.

"I'm sorry Luta, but I am not in town today—and won't be for another week." A lingering silence on the other end told me she had either hung up or was too dumb-founded to reply. "Are you still there Luta?"

I listened to yet more silence and I was just about ready to hang up when I heard a cough and a snort, and then her voice again, exclaiming, "I cunnot vait fur you be home. I need dees answer to dees questin bout me."

Taking a slow deep breath and feeling as though this woman was not listening, I undertook my best effort to accommodate her, "I will try to answer your question now if that is what you would like."

Chapter 21 • Worst-Case Scenario

"Tank-you, tank-you," she said, "Dis ease vat I vant."

I sat back down on my blanket ready to listen to this woman's story, but what I heard was not a story at all, it was just one question—one question that took my breath away. It was a question I had never before heard, and it still runs shivers down my spine when I think of the pain this poor woman must have been going through. On top of this, there was the anxiety of finding me and asking her fateful question. Luta was straight to the point though, and as concise as six words. Six words that I will never forget. Her voice was anxious and strong.

"Vhen do you see me die?"

Rubbing my brow, I was taken by surprise simply by the bluntness of her question. I quickly tried to summon my angels and ask for their help.

"Luta, what makes you feel that you are in danger of dying?" I asked, as I did my best to focus in on her energy. With this heart wrenching question at my feet, I began to get a clear vision of this woman as she emerged from the fog and mist which was until then shrouding her identity from me. I could now see her. She was sitting in a wheel chair, handicapped with a disfiguring life-threatening disease, and one I could sense she was quite tired of being a prisoner of.

I heard her voice fading in and out as she began to tell me, "I eem old, dear. Tire, and in mooch pain. I connut valk yah—have not good life. Please, can you till me when vill I be out dees pain, and out dees world..."

Before I could get my thoughts together, let alone say anything, she carried on with, "I nut fraid to die. I vant to die vor many years now. I don't vant live no more in dees condeeshun. I vant to go be vith God, and my husband. I vill be happy eef you jost till me vhen my life is dun...can you please till me vhen?"

Although still in a half-state of shock, somehow the words suddenly came to me, "The day God is ready for you to join him—this will be the day you will go to be with him. I don't know when Luta, because I am not God, and I do not know what day God has chosen for you to join him in heaven."

"But you are de psychic lady, yah?" she stated matter-of-factly, in a sharp demanding tone. "You can till me vhen I going to die. Dis ease all I vant to know."

"No, I'm sorry Luta, but I cannot answer this question for you. I can't tell you something I simply don't know, just to make you—or anyone—happy. I can only tell you of messages that I receive." I could hear the hollow ring of disappointment and frustration in her voice.

My vision of this woman remained steady and clear. In a wheel chair and knurled up with joint damage to her hands and hips, likely from Rheumatoid arthritis, I sensed her pain-level was over and above what a person should have to endure in this life.

"I'm sorry Luta," I said, choked up, thinking of her troubles, "I feel bad for the pain you are in, and I know that you are ready to cross over to the other side, but I don't feel you leaving this world quite yet."

After a short silence, I had the feeling Luta was wiping away tears. Sadly, I couldn't offer her the forecast she was seeking, and I was sure she didn't much like what I had to say. I then had a vision of her son. His name too; it was David. I surprised myself by how suddenly I could sense how much he needed her, but I also had a gut-feeling Luta didn't want to hear one word of it. She kept saying over

Chapter 21 • Worst-Case Scenario

and over again, "I jist vant to die. I'm ready to go, vhy can't you understand dees." She was getting very upset, talking louder into the phone, and I began to wonder where all this was going to go.

As her poignant words echoed in my ear, a shiver rippled down my back. The sensation vanished as quick as it had come and ended with one of the most serene and calming visions I have ever had. It was of a beautiful rolling meadow in various shades and contrasts of green. The breeze-swept grasses were peppered with endless constellations of those tiny white and yellow wildflowers you see in the spring time. A vivid rainbow arched in triumph over this idyllic landscape. And then, suddenly, there she was, in the meadow itself. As she came into focus I sensed that she would not be crossing over to the other side just yet, even though she was almost willing herself to pass over. So without any hesitation I said, "Luta, I know you are ready now, and your wanting to leave this beautiful earth, but I don't see you leaving just yet, and—"

Before I could tell her about what I had just seen, she cut-in with another phrase I had never before heard.

"You dun't know vhat ease like vhen darknass ease your best-friend, and pain ease your vorst enemy. Sorry to ave bothered you—you deedn't make me veel bettor," she said, with obvious sorrow and disappointment.

Before I could reply, I heard a click and the line went dead.

As I flipped my phone closed, and threw it in my bag, my heart sank at the thought of how I had managed to disappoint this poor lady, by not telling her what she wanted to hear. But, I was at least satisfied that I had been nothing but honest with her. This is all one can do. And, it was no surprise to me when I could hear my angels telling me, "You told her what you were supposed to tell her."

I lay back down on my blanket and closed my eyes hoping to re-ground myself with the beautiful day. What I really wanted to do was just unwind, relax, and soak up the rays of the sun but, somehow, I kept hearing Luta's desperate and despondent words, "Vhen I going to die?" I began to wonder if I shouldn't just pack up and leave the island on the last ferry and go visit Luta in person. I could possibly be of more help to her once I met her. It seemed that now my brain was no longer in any kind of vacation mood, or mode. Even though the call itself had been brief, I somehow knew I needed to go back home and help this poor lady to the best of my abilities. As short as it was, the conversation had already made an impact on my life. However, after talking to friends over dinner about my midday phone-call, they eventually convinced me to wait until the weekend was over so, that I could enjoy two more days of Vancouver Island serenity. Their opinions—and pragmatism—won me over.

The two days flashed by and I bid my good friends farewell. The ferry ride across the inlet was relaxing and enjoyable. I was keenly aware however that I was noticing anyone and everyone who was confined to a wheelchair in a whole different light. Whether they were men or women, young or old, I couldn't help but feel even more sympathetic to their plight. During the passage, I kept wondering why I was the chosen psychic Luta had come to put her faith in. I kept asking myself that stereotypical question, "Why me? Was there a lesson in this somewhere for me? And, if so, what was it? Was I to have told her something I haven't? If there was something, why hadn't I gotten the message yet?" The answers to these questions continued to elude me nonetheless I was determined to find out more about 'the woman who wanted to die.'

After unpacking and getting settled-in back at home I

Chapter 21 • Worst-Case Scenario

checked the calls that had come in while I was gone. As usual, I was swamped with phone messages. About halfway through them I heard the voice of none other than Luta herself. It was a message she had left before I had talked to her that afternoon on the beach. She was inquiring as to whether or not I made house calls and she left her address and phone number for me to get back to her. I listened to her message several times more to see if I could pick up anything else from her voice and, not surprisingly, I did. I genuinely felt that I was meant to pay her a visit, so without wasting any more time I dialled her number. It was then that I realized I was destined to meet this woman.

"Allo, dees ease Luta." she said, with the now familiar German accented broken English.

"Hi Luta, this is Mary," the psychic reader you were talking to a few days ago. How are you doing today?" I said, knowing what her answer was going to be, but asked anyway.

"How nice you call me, vhere you are now?"

"I am here in Kelowna now Luta. I would like to come visit you one day so that I could meet you. We could talk in person, if that is okay with you."

"Tank-you, tank-you," she said, with a heavy but slightly happier voice. "I pray dees to happen you know.

I like for you very much to come see me and ve talk. Dees ease good for me. How you fur tomorrow. My nurse comes fur me in morning, yah, but you come in afternoon. Dees is good fur you? You ave address my house?"

"Tomorrow afternoon is fine Luta. I can make it over for two o'clock, and yes, I have your address from the message you left."

Tank-you, tank you. I vait fur you tomorrow in afternoon. I leeve door open fur you."

"Okay Luta," I said, "I look forward to meeting you. See you at two."

By two o'clock, almost on the nose, I was standing at her front door wondering why she wasn't living in a facility for handicapped elderly people who are unable to care for themselves. Her instructions on the phone were that I was to walk in as the door would be left open for me. Nonetheless, I still felt somewhat like an intruder. I could hear the television blaring away and it was likely she wouldn't hear me knocking anyway, so I decided to simply go in as she requested. I entered slowly so as not to startle even a mouse, and called out her name loud enough to out-decibel the noise of the action-movie in the background. And then, I saw her.

Horrified, I found Luta slumped over to one side of her motorized wheel chair. She seemed to be completely lifeless; she was white as a ghost, and her mouth was wide open. My heart sank and I began to feel faint. I was hoping I would not pass out. My first thought was to call 911 to dispatch an ambulance. My second thought was, *if she was dead, what am I doing here? How could I reasonably explain the truth? I would more than likely be taken in for questioning...*

I quickly set my purse down and went over to her in attempt to determine if she was breathing, or had a pulse. In a panic I gently shook her arm as if to wake her from sleep, shouting, "Luta! Luta!" but there was no response. I could feel my heart pounding as I continued in vain to call her name. Finally, I yelled louder, "Luta, can you hear me?" I must have said it loud enough to wake the dead because she jumped a good inch off her chair and let out a startling

Chapter 21 • Worst-Case Scenario

groan. It sounded as if she was suddenly being attacked. She coughed, cleared her throat and made another groan only this time she opened her eyes. She then looked into mine. There was at first some uneasy trepidation and confusion and then, seconds later, she became calm.

"I am Luta. Pleese vont you seet down." I exhaled with welcome relief. I felt my color, my composure, and my breathing coming back to normal. I found a chair that I could pull close to her wheelchair and, as I did, I noticed there were no pictures or any other personal effects anywhere throughout the room. The place had a distinct cold clinical feel to it and only prescription bottles, syringes, unread newspapers, and mail lay about. I reached out to shake her hand. She offered both her hands, but with closed fists, and said, "Sorry I nut hable shake hands vith you, my hands are too mooch pain. Eet ease nice fur you come visit me. Tank-you. I need only know vun ting." she declared, as she had so many times before. "Vhen I going out dees vorld? Please till me ease soon, I vant be out of pain yah."

Since I had never had any kind of experience with this before, I didn't know what my capabilities as a psychic were, let alone my responsibilities. I asked spirit and my angels for their guidance at that moment, and again they came through for me when I needed them most. "She deserves nothing less than your sincerity and truthfulness. Help her to the best of your abilities."

Remarkably, looking at her face told me much of the story itself. A hard life could be seen beneath the weathered and arthritic features of the poor woman. I knew she was not only ready to go, but was in fact wanting to go. She had been ready for a very long, painful time. What troubled me was how I was going to tell her news she didn't want to hear—that she was *not* going to die quite yet. I kept searching for an answer but every time my angels answered back with, "You have to tell her what you feel."

Softly, and with due respect I spoke. "Luta, I have never been asked this kind of question before—not in all my years of reading."

"Tell me vat you see, she said as tears began welling up in her eyes, "I need know vat you see."

Taking a deep breath, I could sense my spirit guide, Rosa, right beside me saying, "It's alright, go ahead—tell her what you see."

Before Luta could ask another question, I started in on my reply. "Luta, you have three devoted angels around you."

"Oh, dees I know. I ave alvays angels vith me fur very long time."

"You have one on your left shoulder, your mother. The one standing beside you, to your right, is your father." As I spoke these words, a streak of yellow-orange dramatically filtered into the room through a tall south-facing window to the left of us. And in that ray of up-lifting light, I had a vision of a little girl dressed in a plain-white, loose-fitting camisole that went almost to the floor. I knew this had to be her child as a girl whom she had yet to mention.

I was in complete awe of the sudden blast of beautiful sunlight. It seemed somehow as if this beam of light was in someway relevant to leading Luta home. It was a moment I will never forget, of that I'm sure. The ambient energy was simultaneously magical and spiritual. I knew in my heart this was a ray of light from the heavens above—just like it was the day of my father's funeral, telling us everything is going to be okay.

Chapter 21 • Worst-Case Scenario

It wasn't long before Luta asked me, "Who dees be, my udder angel ? You say dare ease tree, ?"

"Yes, you have three angels Luta, and the angel I see on your shoulder is the little girl you lost."

"Yes dees I know. Chee ease on my right shoulder. I carry her alvays dare."

What happened next was quite remarkable. The rays of golden light faded away just as suddenly as they had appeared. As the sunlight vanished, so did the questions that Luta had been asking so desperately before. She never asked again from that moment on. It was as though Luta got touched by an angel that day, which gave her some kind of peace. It was clearly evident she had a curious smile and a calmness about her that was certainly not there when I first walked in. As you can imagine, it was a welcome relief for me that she had ended her heart wrenching questions, about when she was going to die.

It was the following spring when I was flipping through the newspaper looking for some patio planters when I noticed the obituaries. Inexplicably, I had a very strong feeling I was going to see the smiling face of Luta in black and white print. Sure enough, there she was; looking peaceful, happy, and finally with all her loved ones. Looking at her picture with affection, I said under my breath, "You're finally at peace with your angels, I am glad to have met you, Luta."

Chapter 22

The Wedding That Wasn't to Be

I decided that if the phone rang one more time I would let it go to the answering machine because the peaches I had blanched and peeled were turning black by the minute from sitting too long in the bowl while I was yaking away on the phone. But, for some reason, when the phone did ring again I could sense that it was someone who really needed to talk to me. I quickly grabbed some paper towels for my sticky fingers and answered it.

"Hi, is this Mary?"

"Yes, this is she," I replied, trying hard to identify the voice.

"Do you know who this is?" the cheery little voice chimed.

"Keep talking," I said, as I changed ears to hone in on hopefully a better clue.

"I haven't seen you for about twenty years," was the reply.

And then it dawned on me—as soon as those words were out of her mouth, I recognized the voice of a girl who I once baby-sat in North Vancouver some two decades

Chapter 22 • *The Wedding That Wasn't to Be*

earlier. Many people have a captivating look, while others have a captivating voice. Her captivating quality was definitely her voice.

I knew we would have lots of catching up to do, but my inner voice was telling me she wanted and needed to have a reading in the worst way, but for some strange reason was hesitant to ask for one. Picking up on my intuition, and feeling sure I was right, I asked, "Do you remember when you were quite young, when you wanted me to read your tea leaves?"

"Yes," she laughed. "But you said I was too little."

"Well I'm sure you're not too little anymore. I'm going to give you a complimentary reading since you had to wait so long.

"Oh thank-you," she cheered. "You must have read my mind, because that is what I was calling about—to see if you were still doing readings. If I could book an appointment..."

Before I could say anything I heard a voice in my ear saying, "You can read her today."

"Well, let me see," I offered, looking at the mess in the kitchen. Peach juice was now streaking down both my arms and making steady progress towards my elbows. Again the same whisper as before, "You can read her today."

Before I knew it, the words, "Yes you can come for a reading today," came flying out of my mouth.

"That's perfect, thanks! I'm flying home tonight, and was hoping to be read before I leave, so this is wonderful. I have your address from the phone book, and I can stop by anytime that's good for you."

"Let me see," I said as I took a quick look at all the peaches that were still sitting in the sink waiting to be scalded, peeled, pitted, cut and processed. "How about, in an hour?" I said, wondering where the heck my words came from.

"That's fine for me too," she answered, enthusiastically. "I will see you then."

Hanging up the phone, I knew I was in for a race against time. So much to do and so little time to do it in. *What was I thinking?* I thought to myself, *saying an hour and not two! I must be nuts to take this on being as I am, up to my elbows in hot syrup and peaches.* As I soldiered on and rushed through the processing, I began to feel stressed about the time constraint I had set upon myself. Likely not more than a minute or two flew by before I threw my hands up in the air and asked Rose, my angel, "Why did you tell me to take this appointment in the middle of my canning. I doubt I'll be finished in an hour and I can't stop right in the middle of it either. What am I to do?" I asked in a huff.

Minutes later, I thought the planets themselves had conspired against me to slow me down even more when I heard a knock at the door. I opened it blindly and was relieved to find my neighbor and good friend Kaye standing there.

"Kaye, you are a God-send," I cried out. "Can you help me peel some peaches, and get them into jars—I have a client coming by in half an hour, and I will never be done in time. I'm in panic mode!"

"Well actually, I *can't* help you right now, I'm sorry. I only came over to tell you we are going to be away with our horses for the weekend; we were wondering if you could keep an eye on our place while we're gone."

"Of course I can do that Kaye."

"Well, I can see you're in a hurry so I will let you get back to it—sorry I'm unable to help you right now."

Chapter 22 • The Wedding That Wasn't to Be

At that, I bid her goodbye and she closed the door behind her. I literally ran up the stairs three at a time, and focused on the peach canning marathon before me. I had no sooner got to the top of the stairs when I heard the door once again. "For gosh sakes," I exclaimed out loud, "surely this isn't Natalie already!" Then, a louder knock than the one before. Performing as much as a pirouette at the top of the stair landing, I happened to glance in the mirror as I did so. I was none too happy to see that the steam from the canner had melted my mascara off, and matching black smudges under my eyes were the result. For appearances sake, it probably looked like someone had taken a swing at me in a bar-fight.

I opened the door to see my dear, long lost, but not forgotten friend, Natalie. We hugged and rejoiced, laughed, and hugged again.

"Mary, have you been crying?"

"No, I've just been steamed. I'm canning peaches."

"I love peaches! Let me see what you've got going."

"I'm half-way done, more or less. Come on up, I'll show you."

"I remember you reading tea cups when I was just a kid, but I didn't really catch on in those days, too little I guess. I just remember you always putting the tea on—I was mesmerized by you then, and still am now."

She was just as beautiful, energetic, and outgoing as I remembered her. Here was a vivacious girl, full of fun, playfulness, and a joking persona too.

"Will you have time to give me a reading today?" she asked anxiously,

"Sure, we'll make time. What kind of reading do you want Natalie, cards or tea-cup?"

"You decide. I'm not going to tell you anything about what's going on in my life, because I want to see just what you can pick up. Do you really need the tea cups though—or the cards? If you're a psychic, how come you can't just read me straight-up?"

"I don't necessarily need the cups, or the leaves, or the cards or anything really. They are merely tools or elements that my messages can come through, simply because your energy is associated with them."

"You mean you pick up my energy through the cup?" she asked as she pulled out a *Benson & Hedges*, and asked for an ashtray.

"Hmmm, I see then I will have the tea cup reading."

We sat down in my sunroom where I did most of my readings. It was private, cozy, bright and relaxing, I lit the candle, and while doing so had an inexplicable urge to smudge some sage that was sitting upon the window sill. It was a fresh bundle that one of my clients had wrapped for me from the Kelowna foothills that summer. As we sat chatting away, I told her about my life as a childless women and how much I loved kids. Out-of-the-blue, I started feeling uneasy but managed to keep my composure. Natalie finished her tea and turned her cup upside down—the way she had been shown when she was just a kid—and turned it around three times, counter-clockwise. She did this so heavy-handedly, I thought the china cup was going to break.

"I see you starting up your own business at home; a service of some kind for women. I'm getting images of pedicures, facials, massages and the likes."

"Do you mind if I write things down?" she asked. Before I could answer and, moving at a squirrel's speed, she

Chapter 22 • The Wedding That Wasn't to Be

picked up my clipboard and started scribbling away as fast as she could. I could tell by her smile, that what I was saying was making sense to her.

"Very interesting . I have actually been thinking of doing this."

"I see a church…"

"Oh great, I knew you would see it."

Not asking her what she meant, I continued with the reading. "I see tears around you." Suddenly, I had a vision of a cross and I showed her how clear its image showed up even in the leaves. She agreed that she could see it clearly as well.

"I wonder what it means—do you know?"

Taking a slow but deep breath, and ignoring her question, I continued. "I can also see beautiful flowers, a fair number of them too." I knew almost instantly what the cross meant, but didn't want to elaborate on it. "I see a room full of people; family and friends, all together."

"I'm pretty sure I know what all these things are in reference to, but, I want to wait until you are finished before I tell you what I think they mean." This went on for another half hour and when the reading was finished, Natalie announced, "I'm going to tell you about my life now."

"Great I said, I want to hear all about it."

Her expression grew sombre, as she said, "I am engaged and will be getting married in two months. I'm a little disappointed you didn't pick up one thing about my wedding."

I looked at Natalie and said, "I know you are engaged; I could feel that. Besides, I or anyone else would know simply by the presence of that big rock on your finger. It's not easy to hide a diamond ring, especially the one you're wearing."

She laughed as I reached for her left hand and commented on her fiancé's good taste. The ring really was stunning, but as I touched it, I felt sure there would never be a wedding band or ceremony to go along with it.

As Natalie sat their fidgeting with her notes and tapping her toes on the floor, I recalled the familiarity of these habits years ago when she was a little girl. It was satisfying to see that throughout all the years, and all the water that went under the bridge, she was still the same Natalie I remembered.

"I'm still mystified why nothing about my wedding came to you." Before I could answer, she was looking over her notes saying, "Well, you did see some things, let me zero-in on one thing here…umm, oh, yeah—you mentioned a church, undoubtedly the one we will be getting married in." Twirling her hair, she continued down her notes; "Tears? Well that will likely be those of my mom and dad—when they see me walking down the isle. Not to mention myself! Flowers? I'm guessing this must be the bouquet I'll be carrying. Now, regarding the cross, I'm not sure what that could be in reference to exactly, but I do have a cross-pendant necklace; maybe I'm supposed to wear it for my wedding day." She then began folding up her notes and stuffed them into her big cherry-red purse that matched her cute little pump heels in the exact same color.

"I'm just baffled that you didn't see anything else about the wedding. I thought my whole cup would be about it; my honeymoon too. We're going to Hawaii for that—Waikiki Beach for two weeks! Tell me, you didn't see any palm trees or sandy beaches, did you?" Laughing out loud, she added, "Mary, you didn't pick up so many of the things that are in the making right now. You might want to consider finding another career path."

Chapter 22 • *The Wedding That Wasn't to Be*

My wavering uneasiness was now transcending into guilt. I asked spirit once again for a promising answer.

"Natalie, I know you wanted me to see the wedding—of course you would. But if I can't *see* a wedding, then I can't see a wedding. I can't just make it up, just to make you happy? It's not what I do. If I had told you I did' see a wedding, when really I didn't, then I would suffer the consequences if there wasn't one.

"But I'm getting married," she insisted, "in two months, and everything is all in place. We love each other and he's the love of my life. What else can I say?"

"I can see that he really is the love of your life," I said sincerely, hoping she wouldn't ask me any questions about her fiancé Rob. For the rest of our visit we just talked about the good old days, from when she knew me as a flower-child—and one to bake endless batches of cookies and cakes with—to how she met and fell in love with Rob.

Before going out the door, she gave me a big hug, and said, "I'm still in shock that you didn't see my big event. I hope it doesn't mean that there *won't* be a wedding, because my family has spent a fortune on everything. Besides that, people are coming from Germany and from all over the States. I love my fiancé so much. I've never loved anyone like I love him. He is the best thing that ever happened to me, and everyone I know thinks highly of him."

"I'm sure he is a wonderful young man." I said as I got up from my chair and picked up the tea cup. As I did, she glanced at her watch and suddenly realized she was going to be a tad late meeting someone for dinner.

"Gee it's getting late, she gulped. I'm sorry, I have a really important date. Have to run now, and get back to our hotel."

"No problem," I said, relieved that she was leaving, so she couldn't ask me any more questions as to why I didn't see her walking down the isle.

Slipping on my thongs, I walked her to the car and stated sternly; "Take care of you, and let's not wait so many years between visits, okay!" We hugged once more before she began to make her way down the driveway and it was then I noticed tears beginning to stream down her face. I gave her a reassuring smile, took a step back, and suddenly felt a wave of melancholy as I watched her classic candy apple red Honda pull away. A blanket of sadness had loomed down upon me. Intuitively, I knew it would be Natalie who would be telling me of some disappointing news before too long, for she was about to discover that her interpretation of the tears I saw were not tears of joy.

It wasn't long before I got the call I knew I would. Natalie phoned to say, "You were right Mary. I know now why you didn't see my wedding." My heart started to race as I knew she was about to tell me something had happened to her fiancé and that her wedding never took place. "You're not going to believe this," Natalie announced in a sad and distant voice,

"What's that," I answered apprehensively, trying to steady a coffee cup in my free hand.

"My fiancé was in a fatal car accident the weekend before our wedding. The church you saw was the church we held the funeral at. The tears were from those who knew and loved him. Same with the flowers; one sender was as far away as Aspen Colorado. The cross you saw and described is what we have chosen to be placed on the shoulder of the highway marking the spot where Rob was killed."

"Ohhh Natalie...I'm so sorry."

Chapter 22 • *The Wedding That Wasn't to Be*

"I remember being upset with my reading because you didn't see anything about my wedding remember? In fact, I cried all the way home that day, but yet I hung on to the things you did see that seemed related to my wedding. Deep down, my heart was hurting because I thought you must be holding something back. When the accident happened, and I began to think about my reading, I suddenly realized that it was *all* to do with the accident and *nothing* to do with the wedding."

"I'm so sorry Natalie. I wish there was something I could say. Is there anything I can do for you," I offered. "If you need a friend to talk to, now or later, you know you are always welcome here.

Through silence, sniffles, and contained despair, Natalie finally continued to speak. "I'm okay, I think. I have good days and bad days. I'm still in shock to be honest, and the worst is going to be at night trying to sleep, and the first moment of realization again in the morning when I awake. I don't think I will ever get over losing him. We weren't just lovers—we were best friends for over five years."

"I so wish there was something I could say that would help to soothe your soul Natalie. At least try to remember this: God always takes his angels home."

"Thanks for those kind and meaningful words, I will hang on to them" Natalie said gratefully through her tears, "I do believe he was one of them."

"I'm also sure Rob is smiling down upon you, watching over you too. He will forever be sitting on your shoulder—your right shoulder." I was desperately trying to hide the fact that I was choking back tears as well. I managed, but just.

"You know it's interesting to me that you should say that because I feel he is already watching over me, and can feel him right there on my right shoulder—especially when I dream about him. These dreams are so vivid, so real, that when I wake up I can't believe he is really gone."

After the call had ended, I sat there in a daze for the longest time. I was reflecting back on her reading and the fact that I hadn't picked up any vibes concerning the accident. "Why hadn't I," I asked myself. "How did I not see even a glimmer of the accident?" Had I, maybe I somehow could have prevented it. This began to bother me, to the point where I was questioning my own ability as a reader. I wanted to learn, grow, excel and evolve even higher. I wanted to be able to pick up on anything and everything that could even remotely, help or prevent such a tragedy from happening.

I knew of course that for other clients I had not only foreseen impending accidents, but on many occasions where, when, and how. But this one really baffled me, the fact that I didn't get any little piece of it. It only happened one other time that I was devastated beyond words for not seeing an event more clearly. You will read about it in the last chapter of this book.

As the weeks turned into months I continued feeling troubled by my failure to see Natalie's Fiancé's car accident. Guilty even—guilty that I didn't pick up at least something about it. I would often second-guess myself a dozen times or more a day. This went on for almost a year. Luckily—for my nerves and peace-of-mind at least—Spirit would often interrupt my self-accusatory moods telling me, "You were not supposed to see it and, even if you did, it would not have prevented the accident from taking place. God had other plans, and angels were dispatched for him."

Chapter 23

THE SEARCH FOR A DAUGHTER

She was a very sweet little woman whose name was Elizabeth. She had a captivating smile and an unforgettable laugh. I had met her in the late '80s at a friend's home and it was there where she had asked me what I do for a living. When I answered with, "I'm an Intuitive Reader," she made an appointment right then and there and before the week was up she was having her first reading.

"I've never had cards, or any type of psychic reading before," was her first comment the day she arrived at my home. "This will be a new experience for me and I don't really know what to expect."

Smiling back at her I tried to instill some confidence. "I'm sure you won't be disappointed because I feel you were guided to meet me last week. And I also believe you were meant to come here today."

"Well now you've got me really excited," she chimed as she sat down in front of the window overlooking the garden. "What a beautiful and peaceful place you have here." Not being able to sit still, she jumped up in spritely fashion and began walking about the room as if in a daze. "Your home feels so serene and tranquil; you must be able to spend hours in this beautiful reading room just meditating and relaxing."

The sun was streaming through the wall to wall windows, and the fragrance of fresh cut roses and lilacs that I had throughout the room had a combined aroma that reminded me of the sweet tropical air of Kaui. With a pen and notepad on her lap, she sipped her tea and looked my way in anticipation. Through this woman's eyes, I could sense the emptiness she was harbouring even before I had started her reading. My vision was coming more and more into focus. As in so many times before, there was that television-like vividness to it. "I can see a little red wooden wagon. There are four small children inside it and a bigger child is walking alone behind it." Listening intently, and wasting no time in scribbling things down on her notepad. She sat quietly and captivated as I continued describing what I could see.

"It's a girl," I announced, with the same degree of excitement a doctor would have delivering a new baby. "She is your first child and she is not with the others." My fingers and toes were tingling and from out of the blue I saw her name. Roberta!! Her name is Roberta."

"Oh my gosh, oh my gosh," Elizabeth cried out. "I can't believe you picked up her name!" Gingerly handing me her tea cup—as if not to distract my vision—her mesmerized state had suddenly turned into one of infatuated excitement.

"Keep going, keep going—I want to know everything." I knew at that instant that this girl, who was not in the wagon, was a child she had to give up as a baby. I felt this child's energy so strongly that it was as though she was sitting in the room with us.

Chapter 23 • *The Search for a Daughter*

"I see this child in her forties now. She often thinks of you, I can feel it. I'm also getting the feeling that she is perpetually on your mind."

Wiping away some streaming tears she replied, "It's amazing that you can not only see my first daughter—the baby girl I had no choice but to give up for adoption when I was so very young—but that you came up with her name too. What can you tell me about her Mary?"

"Well..., I see you finding this daughter actually."

"You've got to be kidding," she exclaimed, choking back obvious emotions. "I've been looking for her for over forty years now. I have yet to have any luck, and even though I thought I would never give up searching for her, I'm getting tired of constantly being disappointed. The pain, well, it's just been getting too great. Every time I get my hopes up of finding her, I end up losing that much more hope when I don't. Sometimes I think I must be living in a dream-world, thinking that my search will one day lead to her. It is a dream that will very likely never come true and it saddens me so. What I find so fascinating is that I never came here today to ask you any questions about this part of my life but, since you have picked up on such an important and missing piece of my life, I'm beginning to believe that there really must be a reason I came here today."

"You have to believe that you will find her Elizabeth," I encouraged, as I stared into space trying to keep the vision from fading.

"Are you sure she is still alive?" she asked, nervously.

"Yes, she sure is alive!" I answered, handing her a box of tissues. In fact, I see her as healthy, married, and with children, although I'm not sure how many. She must be living somewhere on the prairies as I see endless tracts of flat farmland. I see wheat and grain elevators towering over a frozen horizon. She is living in a place not far from where you gave her up."

"Mary, are you sure of all this?"

"Yes I am very sure, but you will have to go to the little town where you gave up your baby. There you will find a building, perhaps a convent, and the doors will open for you. Archived files in this small town will be your compass, and I see you reuniting with your daughter by the end of the year."

"By the end of the year? But...I can't... I mean...I don't think we can go again, because we actually just got back from this little town. We only go once or twice a year"

Smiling I said, "Never give up your dreams, no matter how unrealistic you might think they are at the time. Anything worth dreaming is worth getting. My advice to you is simple; you must pack up and go again." I looked into her eyes and they gazed back at me with a rejuvenated sparkle. It seemed as if a thunderbolt of energy had just raced through her from head to toe. My steady confidence in the belief that her daughter would be found was beginning to sink-in.

"Get the ball rolling in the right direction at least," I said with an encouraging tone in my voice.

"Well I'll see what my husband says about going straight back again, but I just know he won't share your enthusiasm. The searching we have already done has definitely worn him out terribly. He's tired, getting old and not in the best of health."

"You will leave on a Friday, and come back on a Friday," I said as if I was reading her calendar. "This gives you an entire week to enjoy your children once again"

Chapter 23 • *The Search for a Daughter*

After wiping away a stray tear she asked the question I was waiting for, "What if we go again, and still don't find her?"

"I doubt very much that you will find her on this next trip Elizabeth, but you must return there if you want to find your daughter by year's end. Making this trip facilitates finding her on the next one." I helped her with her coat, took a long, deep breath and added, "Keep positive and think of what you might say to her when you see her." I gave the now re-energized Elizabeth a hug on her way out the door, and wished her a safe journey on the highways. "Try to take some photos and document the trip!"

"I always do write down everything, so I will for sure take notes and I'll phone you as soon as we get back."

Three weeks went by, and there was no word yet from Elizabeth. I did however have a vision of her from seemingly right out-of-the-blue one day while driving to work. It was a vision of Elizabeth hugging her long-lost daughter with her siblings alongside. Everyone was standing around a country-styled kitchen table laden with German food. I was so excited to have seen this vision, it not only cheered my spirit instantly, but I knew then that they had endured another trip to the prairies. All I wanted to do at that moment was share it with Elizabeth, because I knew she would be so excited just to know I seen them all together. My vibes told me that she and her husband were enroot back home. I couldn't get focus, or depth, on their particulars, only the image of the two of them enduring a frustrating drive across the prairies, with disappointment in their heart.

I had a very clear message and vision come to me a few days later while I was pouring my first cup of coffee I could see a stack of papers in my vision. "Elizabeth needs papers!" I told myself, "But what kind of papers?"

"Medical papers," I heard as loud and clear as could be. *Hmm, medical-record papers,* I imagined. I was now lost in thought over the potential such an interesting clue might offer. 'Why didn't I think of this before?' I took another sip of coffee as I began to realize this would be the answer to Elizabeth's prayers. I walked towards my phone-desk, ready to grab the phone-book off the shelf. Just as I opened it, the first ring of an incoming call caused me to jump. My heart I'm sure skipped a beat because I knew it was going to be Elizabeth. I closed the phone book and lifted the receiver.

"Hi Mary. It's Elizabeth; we're back from Regina." Her voice sounded sad, quiet, and disappointed. "I just wanted to give you an update on our trip. I hope you're not busy with something."

"No I'm not busy at all, and I'd love to hear all about it," I said, sitting back down on my chair. I knew that what I was about to hear would not be the news she wanted to relay, or the news I wanted to hear.

"Well, I must say that we had a good time visiting my family," she said with a sigh, "but the place where you told me to go to find my daughter—the old convent—is no longer there. It's now the site of a new office building. We didn't know where else to go to dig up any information, so we decided to come back a bit early and try again in the spring when the weather is good."

"I'm sorry to hear that the trip didn't pan-out for you," I said with sympathy, "but you can't wait until spring—you have to find her before the end of this year."

"Hmm," she huffed, "I just don't know anymore Mary. I'm losing hope. It was a long, tiring, cold and disappointing trip. Worse, Jim is convinced we won't be finding her anytime soon, or maybe never.

Chapter 23 • The Search for a Daughter

"But you have to go back there Elizabeth, and more importantly, you need to see a certain woman who works in an office there. She is the key to finding your daughter.

"Oh no, Mary it's been too much; I don't think the two of us are up to it and I'm quite sure we won't be going back for a while now," she said in a very sad and hopeless tone. "Jim hates driving in the winter, and it's already mid-October. I understand you are convinced, but we just can't go all the way back to Regina like it was across the street. It's a two day trip for us! And as you know, the roads can be treacherous at this time of year." And, before I could speak, she said with a crack in her voice, "I guess part of it is that we just don't want to be disappointed again. It's been over forty years of searching and wondering and hoping—and we aren't exactly young any more."

"Well Elizabeth," I said, "I see you going again within six weeks. Only this time you will be going to a big brick building with a wide and steep staircase and double wood doors at the top. You will climb up those stairs and be immediately happy once you discover what is written upon the door."

"Hey wait a minute...you're describing the building that is just up the street to where the old place used to be."

"Excellent," I replied, smiling. "Then you know where you have to go, and this time you are going to be taking with you your medical history from your doctor."

"My medical history—from my doctor—what do you mean?" she exclaimed.

"Well," I said, trying to be more specific. "It looks like a document listing family medical history, hereditary dispositions, and the likes of those types of things. I can even see your doctor writing a note, and attaching it to these papers. These papers are the absolute key to connecting with your daughter"

"But we don't really have any—"

Silencing her in mid sentence, I knew I needed to be a bit more assertive, "You need to get this paper Elizabeth. I'm not exaggerating when I say it is another key to finding your daughter."

"Another key! What do you mean?"

"I mean it in a figurative way, and I'm sure of it. This piece of paper—this medical history document—will open up the next chapter of your life Elizabeth."

"Oh my goodness, here we go again," Elizabeth cried out. "I sure hope this time you're right!"

"I know you're disappointed from all the previous trips, and so you should be. But, you must believe me *now* because I can see your daughter and she is a beautiful looking woman. She is tall like you, blond, blue eyes, very hard-working, loves gardening. She has loving adoptive parents whom you will soon meet. You are going to find your daughter after forty-five years Elizabeth, make no mistake about it. And, I still say without a doubt that you will find her by the end of this year."

"I'm sorry Mary," she said, shaking her head, "it's just that there have been so many trips and now, look at the date—the year is very quickly coming to an end."

"I know," I said with genuine sympathy, "but somehow this time it will be different. You will have these all-important papers. I'm sorry I didn't get that message before, to save you the trips you've already made, but you have to have faith now in knowing your life-long dream is getting closer by the minute."

Chapter 23 • *The Search for a Daughter*

"Oh, my gosh," she said, sounding noticeably more upbeat, "I just got goose bumps all the way up my arm. I feel better knowing that you see her and that she is still alive. For forty-five years now, I've been wondering if I ever would see her in my lifetime, and now for some reason I actually feel that I might."

"Not might—will!" I said, trying to embolden her confidence. "Someday I will meet her too. I can see her here in British Columbia having a wonderful time with you and, I'm coming over for tea when she does get here, that I guarantee."

"I'm happy, excited, and feel as if I am up in the clouds. Thanks so much for all your encouraging words Mary. Your visions and heart-warming thoughts have helped to restore my hope in finding my daughter. When did you say you see us going back to Regina?"

Smiling I said, "Within six weeks and, I'm sure this time you will come back knowing you have accomplished what you set out to do."

A short silence started to loom, and then the words, "Okay then. I will start preparing for the repack of all our things and convince my poor husband to get ready to set out once again. The first thing I'm doing is calling my doctor's office to put in a request for a copy of my medical history.

"Good for you Elizabeth," I enthused; relieved she was going to return once again. I wished her luck with her husband Jim. To say he wouldn't be too keen on going back so soon would be a colossal understatement.

After hanging up the phone, I had a dream-like vision of this daughter of Elizabeth's appearing as lovely as—and looking very much like—her mother. These exciting images solidified my already steady confidence. *There is nothing to compare to this kind of impending happiness*, I thought to myself!

By early the next morning I was surprised to get the phone call from Elizabeth saying, "Hi Mary. I Just wanted you to know that we've decided to wait until spring until we go back to Regina. Jim has not been feeling all that well, and he doesn't want to make the trip again so soon."

"Oh, but...it's so important that you go. I'm sure once you get the medical history papers in your hands, you will change your mind. I see you going back and finding the place you need to go to. This truly is the key to finding your daughter and it's right at your fingertips. I see you going again Elizabeth, and within six weeks too."

"I'm baffled that you can see us going again so soon after this last trip, especially considering that we're focused on waiting now until winter is over."

"You will be going back before the end of the year, and this time everything will be so much different. I can promise you one thing, you won't be disappointed."

"I have another question before I say goodbye," Elizabeth stated anxiously.

"What's that," I asked, feeling sure I knew exactly what it was going to be.

"Will I get to see my daughter on this next trip?"

Taking a deep breath, I said it as best I could, "No, unfortunately you won't get to meet her on this trip—but I do see you very excited about what transpires this time! I see a very helpful woman phoning your daughter to inform her of you and your papers. How's that for a little bit of inspiration?"

"Hmmm, interesting, so very interesting," she said, listening intently. "And do you still feel that I will find her by the end of this year?"

Chapter 23 • *The Search for a Daughter*

"You will discover her location within a couple of weeks of picking up your medical records. I see you meeting her in person within a month or so after that."

"Oh wouldn't that be wonderful!" Elizabeth exclaimed, with hopeful and high spirits. "You say that with such conviction and confidence that I'm really beginning to believe you."

"Elizabeth, I have seen you meeting and hugging your daughter very clearly! I can feel the tears and emotional release that comes with finally finding each other after so many years. It is going to be the happiest day of your life."

"Oh my. I am so hopeful of all this now Mary. You've got my mind racing. I can't wait to go now. Maybe, just maybe, we could be ready to go by next weekend. I'll let you know what happens in any event and keep you posted on any exciting news."

"Call me if you need to Elizabeth. I'm really excited for you!"

"Wish me luck," she cried out, and the roller-coaster call was over.

It was almost two weeks later when I heard my phone ringing off the wall. The voice at the other end was unmistakably Elizabeth's.

"Hi Mary, we're back once again" she screamed "And we found the right building this time. Isn't that amazing? It wasn't far from where the old building was. Anyway, the lady in charge there took the medical papers from me, and told me that she would cross reference them in the coming days, and let me know if there were any matches to speak of."

"That is great news!" I said, feeling lifted by her enthusiasm. "It certainly sounds like you're another step closer to finding your elusive daughter."

"I am actually getting nervous about the whole thing Mary. I mean, you know, what if she doesn't want me to find her?"

"Now that kind of thinking is not allowed. Keep optimistic! Keep thinking positively." Further words of wisdom for Elizabeth came from those my dad would often expound at home when I was growing up; sayings like "Never give up hope," and, "Where there's a will, there's a way."

"You will hear, within forty-eight hours, something regarding your daughter. It will be by telephone—a woman's voice, asking you questions."

"Are you sure? Then I won't go very far from my phone, because I sure don't want to miss anything. How many more times do you see us going back to Regina before finding her?"

I answered without any hesitation, "I see you going back only one more time, and this time, you will actually meet your daughter in person."

When the phone rang the next day, I knew with every cell in my body that it was her. It was one of those phone calls that you wish you could record, save and keep playing over and over.

"Hi Mary, You won't believe it, I just got a call from the woman I gave my papers to, and you were right. I'm so excited I can't hardy catch my breath. She gave me an inquiry file number and the phone number for the Social Services in Regina. I am to get in touch with them for questions regarding my daughter. Can you believe it? They do know where my daughter is, and now she will know where I am too. The lady has made contact with her, and told me that she wants to meet me as well. This helpful lady is setting up an appointment for a three-way telephone conversa-

Chapter 23 • *The Search for a Daughter*

tion. I'm so happy about all this, yet I still can hardly believe it. I've just called them minutes ago, but they must be quite busy as I had to leave a message at their desk, I'm just on cloud nine"

"Well let's get off the phone then. I don't want you to miss this call."

"I'll get right back to you as soon as I hear from her," she said excitedly.

The next morning I was out in my garden, dead-heading some petunias when I heard the phone. My intuition told me it was going to be Elizabeth with her exciting news, and I dashed into the house almost tripping over my own feet. Out of breath from running the length of our one acre property in just a few seconds, I picked up the receiver. It was indeed Elizabeth. Her degree of excitement was not unlike someone who had just won the lottery.

"Mary—you were right! You were right!"

"Tell me the good news Elizabeth," I said catching my breath.

"Tomorrow I get to talk with my daughter by means of a three-way phone call with a Social Services agent. My daughter is going to be on the line talking to me. Can you believe it?"

"Of course I can believe it." I said. "I knew this day was coming from the first time I ever gave you a reading. I'm so happy for you Elizabeth" It was an immensely satisfying feeling, enjoying the utter sense of relief and happiness my new friend was now experiencing. And, even better, the best was yet to come.

"Mary, I want to thank you for restoring my faith in miracles, and my confidence in myself."

"Did I do both those things Elizabeth?"

"Yes you did, and I will always exalt you for it too. I won't forget either what you told me the very first time we met—about what one needs to do to make a dream come true. You said we need to believe in ourselves. I know now that I will always live by those words because they are so true. You know, I have to keep pinching myself to make sure this isn't all just a dream from which I'm going to suddenly awake from. This is so amazing for me. It is quite a little miracle, don't you think?"

"I'm absolutely thrilled to pieces for you Elizabeth," I said. "I'm sure you will be on cloud nine talking to your daughter for the very first time. Before I let you go, I must give you some much needed credit too. Thanks for having such faith in me Elizabeth."

Two days had slipped by when I got another call from Elizabeth.

"Hello again, it's just me, Sorry to keep bugging you, Guess what? I talked to Roberta on the three-way call yesterday. She gave me her home number so I can call and talk to her privately. She also gave me her adopted mother and father's address, and told me that if I wanted to meet them it was fine with them and with her."

"I'm so happy for you Elizabeth. You've had a long road to travel to get where you are now."

"Thanks for encouraging me to go back again before the spring" Everything worked out just perfectly in finding my daughter before the end of the year"

"Elizabeth, give yourself the credit you deserve as well. You're a champion of tenacity and don't forget it."

"Roberta and I talked about many things as you can imagine and, luckily for me, the rapport between us felt quite natural and genuine. We want to meet as soon as

Chapter 23 • *The Search for a Daughter*

possible, and we're both looking forward to meeting our extended families"

Many years have passed since Elizabeth's remarkable reunion with her first-born daughter. She met all of Roberta's family and to this day still goes to visit her and her ninety-four year old adoptive mother in a rest home in Calgary Alberta.

Chapter 24

THE MURDER

It was the late sixties. I was becoming more and more aware of my psychic abilities. Working in a beauty salon, I was fortunate in that the owner didn't mind if I wanted to read a customer during her hours of business. I was actually getting quite comfortable with this arrangement, and felt I had the best of both worlds—reading people while they were having their hair cut and styled.

This feeling of fun, joy, and comfort was soon to turn into a nightmare however, and I was challenged once again as to whether or not I should continue pursuing my abilities to see future events, or just stick to hairdressing and turn my back on my psychic brain completely.

It happened one day while I was attending to a young lady by the name of Susan. She came in for a particular hairstyle and asked me for a reading while she was under the dryer. No sooner had I sat beside her when I started to pick up some very different visions.

"Who do you know with a gun?" I asked matter-of-factly.

"Oh, my husband has a gun. He and a friend have gone hunting this weekend, so maybe that is the gun you are seeing."

Chapter 24 • The Murder

"No," I said, raising my brow. "The gun I see is not a long-gun, like a rifle, it is just a little short gun."

"Hmm," she said, turning up her lip and scratching her head, "that's called a hand gun. I hope my husband and his friend will be safe on this hunting trip."

"Yes, I said assuredly, "the two of them will be fine. I don't see any hunting or firearm related accident."

"Thank God," she said, "but what else do you see? You can tell me absolutely anything Mary. I want to know it all."

"I see a girl dancing. She is very talented, beautiful, and she loves to dance in front of people."

"Well, that could be anyone of a number of people I know. My daughter loves dancing. I love dancing. My girlfriend is a professional dancer; maybe it is her you are seeing?"

"You have lots of tears around you."

"No, I can't relate to that, although sometimes I cry watching a sad movie."

All of a sudden, my legs started to feel shaky and I didn't want to read her any further. I expediently, but politely, raised the dryer up over Susan's head, and summoned her to my salon chair. It was then that she asked, "Is that it, you can't see anything else? I thought you'd be able to tell me something about my new job, or my marriage, or my kids."

"I can't seem to concentrate right now for some reason."

"Oh...," she remarked, looking as dumbfounded as I was feeling. "Has this ever happened to you before? Is it a normal occurrence?"

"No, not like this," I admitted, with a deep-rooted frown. "I've been hesitant and confused on occasion, but my legs have never gotten shaky and, I have never had a sick feeling quite like this during a reading before."

"What do you think it is—is it me?" she whispered, as she turned in her chair to look me straight in the eye.

"No, it's not you," I confirmed, as I started to remove the rollers from her hair. "It is something to do with this gun."

"You mean the hand gun?"

"Yes, the hand gun," I answered. I know this sounds ridiculously outlandish, but I feel you'll soon hear of a tragedy that will leave you grief stricken."

"Oh my..."

As I continued to comb out Susan's hair, all I could pickup was a vision of her wearing black, as someone would wear in mourning. I kept this feeling to myself. It was enough that I couldn't continue to read her, and because I didn't know what the tragedy was, I felt it would only alarm her further.

"Do you think you could finish reading me next week when I come back for my haircut?" she asked, as she got ready to leave the salon.

"Of course you can," I said apologetically. "I feel terrible about your reading today but I promise I will make it up to you next week."

The following Monday morning while working alone, as I often did on a Monday, I was combing a clients's hair into a big bouffant French roll, when all of a sudden my mind shifted to Susan. I could feel she was in a state of panic, and was going to be calling the salon to tell me something shocking. It wasn't five minutes later when the phone rang, and I almost froze right there where I stood. I just knew it was going to be Susan. I excused myself for a moment, and hurried to the phone. What I heard was something that changed my life forever.

Chapter 24 • The Murder

"You were right Mary. Turn on the radio. A girlfriend has just been shot. She's fighting for her life in critical condition. This must have something to do with the gun you saw. Turn on the radio," Susan repeated, and before I could say a word, the line went dead.

The sound of her voice seemed to echo, a curious occurrence in itself and one which I will never forget. I was so upset that I finished styling my client's hair pretty much as it was and, as politely as I could, got her out the door. At that, I turned the lights out, picked up my belongings, and went home. I simply could not work as my legs were shaking once again, just as they had when I read Susan only two days before.

The next few days were darkened with the news that the girl who was a professional dancer—and a friend of Susan's—died of the gunshot wound. The story was front page in every paper on the newsstand. I was very distraught from it all, and couldn't go to work for the next few days. Although I didn't know the girl, all I kept thinking was, *Why couldn't I see this very terrible murder? Something that bad should have been so clear. Why didn't I finish reading Susan? Maybe if I would have finished reading her, I could have prevented something...*

These questions tormented me for many years. The effect upon me was dramatic enough that I quit reading for seven years after this incident. I moved away from Vancouver, and never wanted anyone to know I was a reader of any kind. My self-imposed exile ended when someone went to great lengths to find me, even after I had settled and got married. It wasn't until analyzing their life's scenario that I considered ever returning to helping people again with intuitive readings. Their story (Chapter 12, *Miracles Really Do Happen*) was one which turned out to be both unbelievably amazing, and heart warming. The happy ending which my psychic abilities afforded, reassured me that my gift of intuition was still relevant, and still helpful. It was then I realized my gift was not something I should ever abandon.

I guess it really is like the old saying goes, "All's well that ends well."

~Janeah Rose, April 30 2012

How To Order Books

Online www.janeahrose.com

see bookstore locations.

www.amazon.com

By email: janeah@telus.net

Methods of payment:

paypal www.janeahrose.com

credit card   phone/E-Mail

Newsletter: stay inspired by subscribing to Janeah's free newsletter on www.janeahrose.com

CPSIA information can be obtained at www.ICGtesting.com
Printed in the USA
LVOW040040051212

309919LV00002B/32/P